D1105952

TENNIS:
How to Become a Champion

TENNIS:

How to Become a Champion

C. M. JONES

FABER AND FABER
London

First published in 1968
by Faber and Faber Limited
24 Russell Square London WC1
Reprinted 1968, second edition 1970
Printed in Great Britain by
Latimer Trend & Co Ltd Plymouth

Standard Book Number Paper edition 571 09415 5
Standard Book Number Cloth edition 571 04714 9

© C. M. Jones 1970

Contents

Illustrations

9

1

The Way to the Top

You want to be a tennis champion, possibly even the winner of the Wimbledon singles.

You may know this, and then again you may not. Perhaps the ambition is so deeply buried in your subconscious or even unconscious mind that you are unaware of it. Yet the mere fact that you are thumbing over this book, or have actually settled down to read it, is clear evidence of your inner feelings.

Maybe the Wimbledon championship lies beyond your abilities. Or, if not beyond your abilities, then beyond limitations imposed by age. Perhaps you have only discovered tennis after marriage and children so that responsibilities of family and business put your deepest ambitions beyond realisation. So be it, but this in no way precludes you from improving very considerably and, more important, deriving more pleasure from tennis than ever before.

There is one qualifying sentence here: if you are a craftsman at heart. Then you will know, or at least be able to sense, the immensely satisfying joy that follows successful completion of a plan that has probed to the limits of your intelligence, skill and effort. Such a joy is so pure and satisfying that it is a complete reward in itself.

There is one other assumption to be made and that concerns your belief that a champion, like a genius, is born of 90 per cent perspiration and 10 per cent inspiration; it must be clear that the perspiration is of the mind even more than of the body. Physical fitness and effort are vital, terribly vital, yet still a small matter when measured against the mental efforts that the average player has to make if he (or she—the use of 'he' from now on infers 'she' also) wishes to improve consistently. It is never too late to improve.

Certainly the most difficult problem that I or anyone seriously interested in teaching tennis faces is the one of building in the minds of pupils a glimmer of what is meant by 'quality of thought and effort'. They hear the words and, in a grammatical sense, understand their meaning. Yet the deepest meaning is so far removed from anything they have ever experienced that one might be talking in Russian or Hindustani.

An article which I contributed in 1964 to *Sport and Recreation*, that thoughtful and stimulating magazine published by the Central Council of Physical Recreation, may help to give some understanding of the quality of thought and effort put out by champions. With due thanks to the editor for permission to reproduce 'What makes a champion', this reads:

'Of the many memories I have of Ken Rosewall, the unquestioned world champion of lawn tennis, none is more vivid than my first meeting with him after he had become a professional at the end of the 1956 season.

'Shy and reserved as a junior and, later, as a teenage phenomenon, his years in the Australian Davis Cup team's iron régime did nothing to remove those characteristics. When, emancipated, he arrived as an individual for the Wembley Professional Championships, he told me of his great happiness thus: "I am married to the girl I love, I am playing the game I love against great players every day and I am earning lots of money. What more could I want?"

'Eight years later and many tens of thousands of pounds richer, Rosewall would unquestionably answer my original question in precisely the same manner.

'Without labouring the point, it is readily apparent to all who know them that Rodney Laver, the world's number two, and Roy Emerson and Fred Stolle, who occupy the first and second positions among the world's amateurs, derive every bit as much pleasure as Rosewall from playing tennis.

'It would be naïve to suggest that their successes—and consequent rewards—play no part in their happiness, but those who have read M. E. Gerhard's "The effect of success and failure upon the attractiveness of activities as a function of experience, expectation and need" (*Journal of Experimental Psychology*) or E. B. Hurlock's "An evaluation of certain incentives used in school work" (*Journal of Educational Psychology*) are likely to share my belief that sheer pleasure in playing tennis may have been an important factor in these men reaching such heights.

'All are Australians. Australia's tennis women occupy a similar position to the men and after four years of failure the juniors Ray Ruffels and John Cooper, representing Australia for the first time, finally wrested the Sunshine Cup from the holders, America, and thirty-eight other competing nations.

'Ruffels is Australia's top ranking junior and possibly the best 18-year-old in the world. He is clearly destined for a major career in the senior game. He is the pupil of Bill Gilmour, an Australian top ten amateur of the Hoad-Rosewall era who later qualified as a coach. He is now one of the best in that country.

'People accustomed to reading about Australian "killer instinct", "determination", "will to win", etc., can be forgiven for believing that all Australian coaching is built upon the development of these characteristics.

'Gilmour, whose eloquence and logic have earned him a place on the Australian professional coaches examining board, denies this vehemently. "Practically all coaching of the 8–13 years old age groups is done in classes of ten," he explains. "At that early age the important thing is to ensure that the youngsters get as much fun as possible out of tennis. Individual coaching is too much for them. They get much more pleasure from group lessons and that way they improve. Those who show promise are given individual coaching after they have been playing in groups two or three years. That is how Ruffels came on and it is the system being used all over Australia nowadays."

'This classical exponent of the "improvement through pleasure" theory includes the other vital requirement for improvement in his curriculum, incentives and targets within the capabilities of his pupils.

'The provision of incentive and targets which are within the capabilities of Gilmour's pupils is in keeping with the findings

13

of Doctor P. Penny when preparing his paper for delivery at the 1965 "Fitness for Sport" conference held at the National Recreational Centre, Bisham Abbey, Berkshire. Doctor Penny spoke on the "good competitor" and based many of his assertions and recommendations on an analysis of the confidential records of combatant R.A.F. bomber and fighter pilots made by the Royal Air Force.

'Among a host of things these reports showed that morale remained high when raids were successful, even when losses were considerable.

'Since success is so important to morale, any training programme should be so graded that the pupil is constantly able to enjoy its success. And even when he or she is defeated, something should be found to praise amongst the many points which might be under criticism.

'If enjoyment of tennis and reasonably attainable targets are important reasons why young Australian players continue to take an active part in the game, it is clear to those who study these things closely that the select few who eventually emerge as champions normally show a tremendous attention to detail which is all too frequent lacking in those who fall by the wayside.

'Three examples emphasize my meaning. The first concerns Rod Laver, who at the end of 1964 ranked number 2 in the world professional game and therefore number 2 in the world as a whole. Laver met Pancho Gonzalez in the semi-finals of the indoor professional championships at the Empire Pool, Wembley, in September 1964. Two and a half hours before his match Laver was found sitting quietly in the dressing-room carefully unwrapping the leather bindings on the handles of his rackets.

'Having done so he patiently laid thin strips of adhesive plaster around the handle and then rebound them with the leather. When I asked him why, he replied, "I find that by making my handles a little bigger it reduces the amount of wrist I use and that makes me more accurate. Against Gonzalez tonight I think that accuracy is going to be more important than the extra speed I get from the use of my wrist."

'Like all the other top tennis rankers Laver gets free rackets and unlimited attention from the company whose equipment he uses. This company would surely have made up the size of the handle for him. But this did not satisfy Laver. He explained, "If I do it myself I get the racket exactly as I want it, even if I have to make several changes. So I would rather do it myself."

'Ken Rosewall, world champion for the past five or six years, presents another facet of this kind of approach. Already world champion a couple of times, Rosewall was discussing his game in the dressing-room at Wembley with Dan Maskell, the L.T.A. training manager, and me some years ago. He asked us if we had noticed anything different about his forehand drive and then went on to explain: "Last year when under pressure I used to take the ball off my back foot and that made me a little uncertain. So I have been learning to take the forehand on my front foot. Don't you think it is very much better?"

'Undoubtedly his forehand under pressure was better, but since not more than two players in the world were then capable of putting him under pressure and he still was able to beat them, he still considered it worth-while paying attention to a detail which no one was really capable of exploiting.

'The third example comes from Pancho Gonzalez who appeared to be serving many more balls across the court towards the end of his career than he did earlier on.

'At that time of his life Gonzalez's English appearances were restricted to the annual championships at Wembley. When asked why he was serving in this manner he explained that the humidity caused by the ice beneath the boards affected the flight of the balls. After elaborating on some fairly involved theory, he concluded that by serving across the court he gave himself a greater margin of safety against the type of returns possible to the receiver.

'This analysis staggered even some of his fellow professionals. Mike Davies, who had just quit as Britain's top amateur to join the paid ranks, exclaimed, "I never knew that. It just goes to show what a detailed knowledge of tennis he has."

'As a final example, consider the case of Jack Kramer, to some experts the greatest player of all. Kramer romped through Wimbledon in 1947 and looked utterly invincible. Not satisfied,

Kramer rose early on the Sunday morning to catch a plane to Chicago where he sought the aid of Bob Harman, one of the deepest-thinking coaches in America.

'There were many men who would gladly have trained the famous Californian just for the prestige but Kramer insisted on paying, his ultimate bill coming to approximately $100. Kramer eventually rectified with Harman the flaw in his cross court forehand drive, a flaw which he reasoned might endanger him should he meet Frank Parker in the American Championships. He did, in the final, winning after losing the first two sets.... And the cross court forehand drives played a vital role in that win.

'This attention to tiny details—and the eagerness to see they are attended to—spreads over into diet. All the top professionals and most of the leading amateurs pay strict attention to the quality and quantity of food they eat. Indeed, Gonzalez and Luis Ayala now restrict themselves to virtually one main meal each day. At other times they eat very sparingly. This contrasts vividly with the words of Dr. A. S. McIntyre at the Fitness for Sport Conference. An expert on nutrition, he reported that in one survey he made among athletes 97 per cent said they paid no special attention to diet.

'Thirty-five years in and around championship tennis have convinced me that attention to minute detail, applied concentration—I dealt with this in an earlier article in this magazine—plus a genuine delight in playing tennis are far more important than any genius for timing and hitting a tennis ball.

'What motivates those who show the determination and drive to take these pains? What is lacking in those who do not? Can this motivation be discovered early in a promising youngster's life? These are all questions which no one in this country yet seems capable of answering.

'Even the stars themselves seem incapable of analysing themselves, for in an extensive poll carried out at three of the major international championships less than 3 per cent of the world's best amateurs named ambition, drive or determination as qualities which had helped them to their positions of eminence. Yet it was crystal clear that all possessed them, in many cases abundantly.

'For that reason perhaps I should not be worried by a snap though admittedly small investigation I conducted among Britain's top juniors in January 1965.

'All said they wished to become top class players but in response to a question: "What do you like best about tennis?" all answered "the social side" and only one added the rider "winning matches".

'In fact several of them are ambitious. Yet don't you, my reader, share my disquiet over those answers "the social side"?'

Before moving on, there is one further point to make. It is best summarised: 'A house is built from many small bricks.'

A beginner has everything to learn and advancement can be rapid if the tuition is skilled. Later, after the basics have been grasped, ancillary strokes queue up to be added and the going becomes a little more difficult. Tactics start to impinge on the mind and this involves thinking of many factors besides strokes.

Once an English player has gained a place in the country's first ten, he cannot reasonably hope to invent a stroke or idea that will suddenly bring dramatic advancement. Attention to detail is what counts. There are very few players who could not seek out and find a dozen or more technical or tactical tendencies or deficiencies which need correction in their games. These details may be so small that they are worth only two or three points each in the course of an entire season. Yet it is a fact that such details usually turn traitors in a crisis and twenty-four critical points won instead of lost in a season can well be worth six places in the rankings.

Rod Laver provided a dramatic example during his 'grand slam' year, 1962, when he won the singles championships of Australia, France, Wimbledon and America. Don Budge in 1938 is the only other man who has ever achieved this, and Laver's feat led to a professional contract that has proved so lucrative that Laver could have retired by the end of 1965, at the age of twenty-seven, had he so wished.

Playing in France, Laver was within one point of losing to Martin Mulligan, but Laver, as you read earlier in this chapter, pays attention to details—including details of the methods adopted by other players. Mulligan is less thoughtful in his play.

Let Laver take up the story: 'Mulligan had been returning my services to his backhand with down-the-line shots. This shot is a favourite with him so I reckoned that if I got in a three-quarter pace first service deep to his backhand, he would play the same shot as usual.'

Left-handed Laver's first service was good and he ran in fairly fast, covering the down-the-line return. The ball came where he expected and he sped a backhand volley across the court well beyond Mulligan's groping racket. Laver went on to win and he said later: 'If Mulligan had returned the ball across court, I would have been deep in trouble'.

The fact is that Mulligan was not thinking; Laver was, and so he won a point which turned out to be worth £45,000 to him; quite a valuable point.

Mulligan's failure on this point also spotlights another vital factor in fighting for improvement. That factor is to dominate the ball and not be dominated by it. Far too many players—perhaps 99 out of every 100—mostly choose the shot suggested by the path and speed of the oncoming ball, rather than the shot which, tactically, should put the opponent in the greatest difficulty.

Before embarking on the main sections of this book, are you convinced:

(1) That over and above any natural physical advantages they may possess, champions show an infinite capacity for taking pains?

(2) That improvement comes most rapidly and consistently when every single shot in each practice session is executed with every ounce of applied thought and controlled physical effort?

(3) That three-quarters of an hour's practice in this way can be twice as exhausting and ten times more valuable than four or five hours of aimless hitting and set playing?

(4) That to obtain the maximum benefit from this book you will have to study it as intensively as you did any of the text-books of your schooldays?

(5) That the recommendations and ideas you accept and adopt must appeal because of their logic and not because this or that champion says they are right?

(6) That you are a unique human being differing in one or more ways from every other human being and, therefore, you must use this book and all other aids as tools to help your individual progress? That you must never become an unthinking slave?

(7) That, above all else, drive and determination will contribute most to your advancement?

(8) That neither I nor anyone else can teach you anything, but only present you with the fruits of our knowledge and experience; it is you who have to LEARN from what is offered?

(9) That no experiment can be a total failure? That the worst outcome leaves one with sure knowledge, instead of doubts about what happens when a particular line of action is taken?

(10) That training for improvement demands total involvement and dedication?

(11) That advancement is attained by a continuous succession of very small steps?

(12) That total involvement and dedication bring many rewards as bonuses—including deep satisfaction—beyond the mere achievement of the ambition and that the journey may be even more pleasant than the final arrival?

If you are, the moment has come to embark on general instruction; but before that, two small caveats about learning.

The first: improvement in tennis does not maintain a continuous upward path. Instead, each stage of improvement is normally followed by a plateau of stagnation or even a regression. These periods can be, and sometimes are, terribly depressing. Often they arise because one is momentarily in the state of having taken in new methods or ideas to the limits of one's capacity and time is needed to absorb them. These are always periods that demand special strength of will and purpose. It is so easy to find the energy and time to practise when flushed with success, and equally easy to go to the movies or a dance when the going on court is tough. It is at these times that the champion shows his true calibre.

The second concerns attitudes on and off the court. Clearly no one will improve his ability to time and hit a moving ball correctly without spending considerable time on court with a friend, coach or opponent. But one also needs ample time for the brain to absorb the points one is seeking to learn. Learning is as much a mental process as it is physical—perhaps more so. Indeed, the famous American psychologist William James states with a good deal of truth, 'one learns to ski in the summer and to play golf in the winter'. This theory, perhaps surprisingly to some readers, is now supported by a good deal of experimental evidence of 'ideo-motor action'.

Briefly, if a subject lies still on a couch, has an amplifier connected to his arm muscles by electrodes and is then told to imagine he is lifting that arm, the nervous impulses passing into the muscles correspond to those which would have occurred had the movements actually been made. So nerve transmission and mental ideas are closely related and it seems one cannot occur without the other. It is entirely logical, therefore, for a determined pupil to 'imagine' himself out of a poorly grooved stroke into one which is technically sound.

With, it is hoped, your brain now fully alerted and active, let us progress.

Starting Point

The art of tennis can be found and mastered by your total personality—this includes your mental and physical aptitudes—working together on three all-embracing facets of the game:

(1) Practice;
(2) Concentration;
(3) Temperament.

Harry Hopman, by now a near legendary figure in Australia and the man most responsible for his country's unequalled record in the Davis Cup, once calculated that success in tennis comes 75 per cent from character and only 25 per cent from strokes or natural ability to produce strokes.

I share this view but this in no way minimises the importance of strokes, especially now that so many major events are contested on slow, red clay courts.

On fast surfaces one can survive through deploying one or more outstanding weapons of attack. Arthur Ashe's and Michael Sangster's crushing cannon-ball services are two dramatic examples.

Slow surfaces sap the lethal power of such weapons, so allowing the more complete but less powerful player to return the ball, gradually build up a superior position and then exploit the weakness. Look at the players heading tennis in 1970: Rod Laver, Tom Okker, Arthur Ashe, John Newcombe, Tony Roche and Ken Rosewall, with Margaret Court, Ann Jones and Billie-Jean King among the women. Though each of them possesses some shots which are better than others, there is not one major weakness to be found among the entire ten of them.

Certainly none of them, when fully geared up and trained for a major event, is likely to be upset on the day by an opponent who notices a pronounced and exploitable weakness.

May it be assumed that you are now intellectually alerted to the importance of possessing an extensive repertoire of technically sound strokes and that stroke play has been put in its correct perspective?

Good, but before moving on to discuss stroke play in detail there are other points to cover. Making a stroke demands a player, a racket, a ball and a court. The player must be clothed. Clothing, rackets, balls and courts vary so let's learn a little about them.

Firstly, clothing. Neat, well—but slightly loose—fitting, absorbent, easily-washed clothes are best. Long experience has convinced me that a clean, well-turned-out player is normally a tidier thinker than his untidy, dirty counterpart. Neat appearance, too, is likely to aid confidence. This applies to women also, and I am equally convinced that the bizarre outfits worn by some—remember Maria Bueno at Wimbledon 1962?—positively invite self-consciousness, surely the arch-enemy of relaxed, easy performance.

So for men an absorbent, drip-dry shirt and drip-dry shorts, for women a similar outfit with, perhaps, a neat skirt replacing the shorts.

Warmth, especially after the heat of battle, is of prime importance, and a wind-resisting sweater or cardigan is a 'must'. Don it immediately after play and always change into dry clothes at the earliest possible moment. From court to changing room should be the inviolable route.

Socks should be absorbent and well fitting—perhaps fractionally on the loose side—and should always be thoroughly clean before the start of a match. Whether thick or thin—this goes for the soles of shoes too—depends on the feet of the individual. Find from experience which suits best.

Shoes are a special problem because differing court surfaces have differing effects on footholds and players vary in the way they run. Some like to be able to slide a little and so are not upset by the slightly slippery surface which is standard for most

British hard courts—they call them clay courts in America and many other countries. Others, including most tall and well-built men, prefer a very solid foothold. On English hard courts this necessitates soles with deep ridges, and the old-fashioned rope-soled sand-shoes still to be found at many seaside resorts are best of all. If possible, buy a pair of these and reserve them for use under exceptionally slippery conditions or where an improvement in foothold can mean the difference between winning and losing.

It is often a good idea to spray talcum powder on one's feet and in the shoes, too.

Always take spare shoe-laces on court, a safety-pin or two and even spare shoes and socks. A rapid change before a final set sometimes works wonders.

So, happy in a neat, clean appearance, one steps on court.

In Britain this will almost certainly be one of four surfaces —wood, grass, red rubble hard (clay), or asphalt. Providing all are equally well cared for, the order shows their order in speed.

The speed of a court is related to the resistance it offers to the ball. Polished wood offers virtually none and short smooth grass (as at Wimbledon) very little.

On the other hand, red rubble offers a great deal, the ball seemingly burying each time before rebounding slowly and high. Asphalt of the type found in many public parks is worst of all.

Simple, if expensive, proof of relative resistance can be found by playing two sets on each surface, using new balls each time. Wood will affect the balls little but asphalt, the other extreme, will make an alarming assault on the nap of the balls.

Thus it is that the tennis at Wembley or Wimbledon is considerably faster than that at Bournemouth, where the famous British Hard Courts Championships are staged, or at Stade Roland Garros, home of the French Championships—the World Championships on hard courts.

These surfaces demand different methods of play but that comes in other chapters.

Legend has it that Henri Cochet, who won Wimbledon in

1927 and 1929, once offered to play the final of an important championship with any racket anyone cared to give him. However, neither he—nor any other champion—would make such an offer with tennis balls.

The controllability of a standard, L.T.A. 'approved' tennis ball is very directly related to the nap of the cover, for this is what gives it most of its air resistance, and air resistance is the handmaiden of control. When developing your tennis buy new balls as often as possible, even at the expense of a top grade racket.

Not that a top grade racket isn't important—it is, very. Choose a racket by feel after making numerous imaginary strokes. Make sure it can be gripped comfortably. Too large a handle leads to tiredness, one too small to muscular tension and even tennis elbow. For safety, buy one of the nationally advertised makes, for they are extremely carefully 'quality controlled'.

Tight or slack, light or heavy? Stiff or whippy? Six vital factors. Which shall be chosen?

First think about this question: 'Can a tennis racket have any effect on a tennis ball except when that tennis ball is in actual contact with the strings?' Clearly the answer must be 'No'.

Consider again: 'Can as much spin or force be imparted to a ball when it leaves the racket face instantaneously as when it dwells on the strings for, say, one-fiftieth of a second?'. Again the answer must be 'No'.

Finally, a dip into mechanics for the factors which make up force. Force, the factor which gives speed, is the result of mass multiplied by acceleration.

Armed with these three items of knowledge, consider now the choice of a racket.

It must be related to the type of game played and this, in turn, is affected by the character and size of the player.

Generally, a large man cannot be so quick and nimble as a smaller man, so he will tend to rely on power.

On the other hand, a smaller, nimbler man may also be very severe; perhaps the severest forehand drive of all time belonged to a man who scarcely weighed nine stones, William M. Johnston.

But if power is the main requirement, a modicum of control will still be essential. And touch players—men like Beppi Merlo and John Bromwich—cannot allow their subtly angled shots to fall below a certain basic pace.

For 'touch tennis' the ball has to remain on the racket strings long enough for its 'feel' to be transmitted and interpreted by the striker's brain. This entails slacker stringing and, perhaps, less mass (weight) in the racket. Bromwich, in fact, used a $12\frac{1}{2}$-ounce racket strung like a 'fishing net'. Merlo too uses a slack racket. Despite slackness, the gut must be responsive (i.e. it must possess good elasticity) and for this top quality natural gut cannot be beaten. I believe it to be important for children to learn with natural gut rackets because they must develop swings in which the racket does most of the work. With man-made gut the youngster will need to use force rather than swing.

However, the cost of high quality and fine gauge natural gut is not only expensive; it also wears quickly, especially in the wet conditions so often found in the British Isles.

Today, nylon and other artificial strings are not a bad compromise, though their poor elasticity, compared with best quality natural gut, demands slightly slacker stringing if the ball is to remain on the strings long enough for either power or control. On balance, it is the power players who suffer most from use of artificial strings, though even this can be compensated for to some extent by increasing the elasticity (whippiness) of the racket frame.

However, increased elasticity in a frame is noticed much more by players than increased elasticity in gut and I know of no top class players who use different frames for different gut.

Acceleration and mass are vital to power and nothing can beat fine gauge natural gut for this. The strings give to the ball and, according to the stringing tension, snap back again to normal at an enormous pace.

Balancing this elasticity with the elasticity of the frame is a highly complex technical problem on which I am not qualified to write. In general, wood does not spring back to its normal state as speedily as natural gut, so in seeking speed think mostly in terms of the gut. The elasticity of the frame, from a practical

point of view, is felt more in the comfort of the racket when in use.

Now steel, streamlined rackets have introduced new dynamics and fresh variables in terms of frame and gut elasticity, weight, balance and stringing tensions.

These problems are well understood by the top, nationally advertised manufacturers, so do not economise more than necessary, and allow the feel of one or other of the top makers' rackets to be the guide, though bearing in mind the general theory relating to touch and power.

3

Choosing a Game

At this stage of the book pause for a while to consider the type of tennis you are probably best suited, physically, mentally and temperamentally, to play.

Broadly speaking, there are four main categories:

(1) Powerful aggression;
(2) Aggression by touch and finesse;
(3) Tactical defence;
(4) Negative, nimble defence.

Strange as it may seem the starting point for all should be the same—the acquisition of ball control. This is not only logical; it has been adopted successfully in actuality by successions of great attacking champions, among them Donald Budge, Jack Kramer, Pancho Gonzalez, Lew Hoad and Rod Laver. All learnt to control the ball before they stepped up speed and all firmly advocate 'control before speed'.

This does not mean, however, that one should remain a 'pat-baller' all through one's career. There is a definite danger of this happening, particularly in boys or girls who learn a lot of their tennis before physical maturity. In junior tennis it is rare to find players with the control, power and knowledge to overcome the speedy, determined runner who is content to keep on pushing the ball back as best he can while patiently waiting for mistakes to come.

Because of this, there is a marked tendency for juniors to form negative playing habits which are extremely difficult to break once they become ingrained.

Winning is vital and, as is discussed later, partially habitual.

27

Nevertheless, one must maintain a balance between the immediate importance of winning a particular match and the longer term need of technical and tactical development.

Since winning is strongly habitual, there should be no question of ever setting aside one's determination to emerge the victor in a match.

The compromise is to decide on a mode of play and to do everything possible to win using that mode. The resultant development of will power—if the mode is inflexibly followed right to the point of self-destruction—is likely to counterbalance the deleterious effect of defeat, providing a genuine effort to win, rather than just to practise, has been made.

To return to the theme of control, in stroke play the most important thing is to put the ball in play. Next, to ensure that it falls on the desired spot. Thirdly, to ensure that it reaches it in the shortest possible time.

The complete player—a man like Ken Rosewall or Rod Laver—can do this with any of a vast range of strokes made from any part of the court.

And this is precisely where the great arguments about the relative merits of natural strokes and those acquired through coaching need very careful study.

I cannot overstress that the vital factor is control. Each player must ask himself clearly and answer with utter honesty the question: 'Can I hit the ball to any square foot of court I desire, irrespective of the depth, speed, angle and height at which it is stroked to me?'

Actually, this is not a question the beginner or average player is capable of answering fully, for the requirements in his class of play are vastly less stringent than those in the top brackets of international competition.

To give a concrete example, it is possible to play a sliced backhand down the sideline which pitches well short of the service line. But it will, of necessity, be far slower in pace than one which dips to the same spot because the stroker applied top spin.

In average tournament tennis this would not be disastrous. Against a top-class opponent with the speedy reflexes and movement of a Roy Emerson or Rod Laver it would be fatal. That sliced backhand would be the target of a net attack and, because of its slowness, would never evade the volleyer; he would gather an abundance of points with scarcely any trouble at all.

So in achieving the prowess to get the ball in play, to the desired spot, and at good speed, it is vital to project one's thoughts forward to the highest level of play one ever hopes to achieve. Bear in mind, too, that ambition normally feeds on success, so think big.

This presents problems of its own, for it is almost impossible for an average player to conceive the speed and power of Wimbledon tennis, especially in its late stages.

That is one of the reasons why so many champions have a coach or friend behind them. At first the coach contributes 80 per cent of the total effort, then 70 per cent and so on down to, perhaps, 20 per cent as the champion eventually reaches his peaks of skill, experience and achievement.

This leads logically to my belief that coaching—good coaching—is invaluable. In sport generally there is a widespread belief that to do what comes naturally must, of necessity, be best. One has only to watch the average beginner to realize that, in tennis, this is scarcely ever true.

Yet in seeking coaching the ambitious player must never abandon his role as principal. In the early stages this role may be very nebular but always he will be the person who plays the matches. No matter how thorough and skilled the advice given to him before he goes on court, or even during the match itself, it is always he who has to overcome tension, tiredness, nervousness, the efforts of his opponent and so on, and put the advice into action.

Therefore, from his very first lesson onwards the pupil must ask 'why', 'why' to everything he is told. He must fully understand what is being taught and why but, above all, his mind must be completely convinced that the advice is right for him.

The pupil must also realize that even the finest coach in the world cannot make him do anything. The coach can teach but the essential action comes from the pupil in learning. Most of the really great champions—men like Bill Tilden, René Lacoste,

Henri Cochet, Don Budge, Jack Kramer, Pancho Gonzalez—were great thinkers about tennis right from their earliest days.

Should a player go to more than one coach? What action should be taken when, once success starts to come, hundreds of well-wishers, cranks, and those who wish to be 'in on the act' start proffering advice?

On the basis of 'out of the mouths of babes and sucklings . . .' listen, dissect, discuss with the coach or friend, and then take the appropriate action—most of the time this will be to ignore the advice.

Occasionally the advice will be good, and it will not always come from an accepted authority. For example, Jack Kramer and Ted Schroeder both profited vastly from a deep knowledge of the geometry of tennis gained from a mathematician who was only a moderate player himself.

On the other hand, Ken Rosewall improved his service markedly after one fifteen-minute spell with Donald Budge; Budge had spotted that Rosewall served with a locked wrist and it took him moments only to get Rosewall to relax his wrist, put more snap into the hit, and obtain more speed.

The champion is always very self-reliant; so acquire that characteristic from the start. Do not adopt new ideas too quickly or, having adopted them, abandon them at the first trace of disappointment. Decisions taken either at the height of happiness or depth of despair are seldom to be trusted.

In the early stages the coach knows far more than the pupil but that must not dissuade the pupil from querying, quizzing and analysing. He must never forget that soon he will be out on a match court very much alone and then all the knowledge and skill he can muster may prove most valuable.

So to return to the opening paragraph of this chapter, learning to control and direct a tennis ball at high speed demands a deep knowledge of what can be developed completely naturally and what must be acquired through professional coaching or with the aid of a highly skilled amateur player and analyst.

The first things to assess are one's ambitions and the opportunity to set about achieving them. Clearly, a man of over thirty with a wife and two children to support cannot honestly aspire to much more than a place in the county team—assuming that his current standard is only good club.

On the other hand, a youth of seventeen who doesn't mind roughing it a bit, who is prepared to forgo preparation for a formal job, who has indulgent parents, and who possesses average talent plus a superabundance of perseverance, intelligence, and industry may reasonably—reasonably, that is, to people who understand the compulsion of sport—embark on a campaign to win a place in his country's team.

In real life, however, the situation is seldom so clear cut as either of these two cases, and many other factors have to be assessed. Perhaps one parent approves and the other does not. More likely, the aspirant to fame lacks the moral courage to cast himself completely adrift before launching himself on a tennis career. The mere fact that he hesitates is a sure indication that he will never succeed; the Kramers, Perrys, Lavers and so on never suffer a moment's hesitation.

So in assessing ambition it is vital to be utterly realistic and completely honest with oneself—an ability only a tiny minority of men are lucky enough to enjoy.

Usually, tennis must be made to fit into a complete life—and, once it is made to fit, it is surprising how much time and opportunity there is. Time and opportunity enough in the case of a few exceptions like Ted Schroeder and Dick Savitt to win the singles at Wimbledon.

In reality, most stars began playing for the joy of tennis, progressed, and one ambition followed another. The decision to try for top honours came quite late.

This injects the task of a coach with a large dose of danger. The popular idea of leaving a player to develop strokes naturally is seldom completely right. Undoubtedly natural strokes are capable of taking the average player a long way, but, having watched hundreds of beginners in my life, I am absolutely convinced that 999 out of every 1,000 need help, either from a professional or skilled amateur. There are inherent tendencies of stroke making in nearly all beginners which can never withstand the pressures of high grade play.

Yet in endeavour to correct or eliminate these tendencies or

31

weaknesses the coach lays himself open to the charge of ruining the pupil's natural style.

Coaches are very mindful of the need to build on what is natural and good while eliminating what is natural but weak. They vary in their power of discrimination and some are carried away by their own enthusiasm. So question a coach when he suggests a change and never believe that eliminating something which seems natural must be harmful.

Yet in deciding to change—or not to change—always relate the decision to reasonable ambitions before coming to any irrevocable decision.

Pose very definitely the question: 'If I do not make the change will I be able to put the ball in play, ensure that it always falls in the target area, and at a pace sufficiently fast to ensure me success in the highest standards of competition to which I aspire?'

On the basis of the answer the decision can be made.

The question of pace in stroke play requires further study. Monotonous returning of the ball may be successful in junior tennis but it does not win the big events; it is necessary to seek a happy medium between this and blind, unthinking slogging.

The danger, especially when meeting a reputedly far better player, lies in attempting to begin and sustain a pace beyond one's natural or developed abilities. I deal with this subject at greater length in the chapter headed 'Pressures and Nerves'. For the moment accept that there is an optimum speed of play for each and every individual. It lies somewhere between the extremes of 'nothing-to-lose' blind slogging and the sheer pat ball of 'no matter what happens, I must not make a mistake'.

Each player, probably with outside advice, must seek ever to increase his optimum pace, not by blind hitting but perhaps through a constant endeavour to take the ball ever a fraction closer to the point where it bounces.

Simultaneously continuous efforts must be made ever to increase the force applied to the ball. This does not come about at all easily. Just as runners find it heartbreakingly difficult to increase their speed—though not their endurance—so ball players meet with numerous problems in seeking added power.

These problems are basically physiological, psychological and neural. Many of them are lessened when the key formula—force equals mass times acceleration—is kept sensibly in mind. Then pace is sought through good swinging and timing (because this achieves racket acceleration plus effective mass and the transference of body weight).

In more advanced stages of development, inquisitive players may like to experiment with wrist snap, because wrist snap, especially when serving, can really make the racket head whistle through the air, so converting a fast shot into a thunderbolt. However, this is so advanced and dangerous a technique that I will not elaborate any further.

A tennis court is 78 ft. long and is separated in the middle by a net 3 ft. 6 in. high at the end sagging to 3 ft. in the middle. Except when a ball is struck above net height from fairly close in, it has to drop in flight if it is to pitch within the boundary lines of the court.

So there is a limit to the speed at which a drive may be hit unless some artificial means of making it drop or dip in flight is found. How this is achieved emerges in the next two chapters.

4

Basic Ground Stroke Theory

HITTING HEIGHT—STAYING WITH THE BALL—GRIP—FEELING

The preceding chapter has shown in detail some of the factors which affect the dynamic behaviour of a tennis ball. This is also controlled very largely by spin and in a later chapter this is covered fully, both in theory and practice.

However, before spin can be applied, strokes must be learnt or developed. So for the moment accept that top spin, or lift as it is sometimes called, causes the ball to dip in flight while slice tends to make the ball rise in flight. Why can be studied later.

From the preceding chapters it can be reasoned that, all other things being equal, the longer the racket remains in contact with the ball, the better will be the control. And even when speed rather than control is the ambition, tightly strung, resilient, thin gut with rapid elasticity is preferable to a board-like, non-giving racket face.

Accepting this, what are the basic requirements for ground strokes?

The natural height at which the majority of top class players hit the ball lies around the waist. In the case of a man 5 ft. 10 in. high, this will be about 2 ft. 11 in. off the ground and, remember, the net which divides a tennis court is 3 ft. high in the centre, 3 ft. 6 in. at the posts.

Since no man in his right senses tries to make each drive touch the net band in passing, some kind of elevation must be given to the average shot.

In men's play this safety margin over the net is likely to vary between 1 and 3 ft., in women's play between 2 ft. and 2 yds.

These heights refer to normal, baseline line rally play. When attacked from the net, the clearance may barely exceed 1 or 2 in.

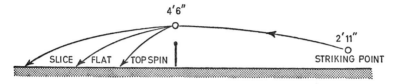

FIGURE 1

Figure 1 shows the flight of the ball after typical ground shots hit with top spin, slice and flat. Slice is obtained by hitting the ball with a downward stroke, the racket face being inclined upwards. This movement imparts the slice.

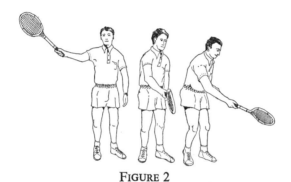

FIGURE 2

Figure 2 shows how the racket face appears during a sliced stroke. Since its direction of travel is downwards and the ball has to travel upwards, the length of time the strings can stay in contact with the ball must be less than in Figures 3A and 3B. This assumes that the speed at which the racket face travels and the tension and elasticity of the stringing are identical.

In Figure 2 the bottom edge of the racket moves forward slightly more than the top, so slicing the bottom of the ball in a forward rotation.

From Figure 1 it can be seen that the normal drive has to be lifted to clear the net.

35

Figure 3 (A and B) shows how the racket face travels in imparting top spin to the ball.

FIGURE 3A

FIGURE 3B

In Figure 3A the top edge of the racket moves more than the bottom, rolling the top of the ball forwards in flight—hence top spin or lift. In Figure 3B top spin is imparted by an upwards brushing action. This is frequently seen at club level. In each case the diagram slightly exaggerates the dynamic action.

If the timing is correct and the gut resilient there will be significantly longer contact between ball and racket than in the slice shot shown in Figure 2.

Since slice causes the ball to rise in flight, while top spin makes it dip, any given speed of drive will make the distance between hit and pitch of a sliced ball longer than the distance between hit and pitch when lift is used.

Thus it is possible to hit far harder with top spin than slice while keeping the ball in court.

36

Furthermore, because of the additional time gut and ball are in contact, any given strength of swing will achieve more power with a lifted stroke than it will with one that is sliced.

The first lesson in ground stroke making, then, is that a slightly lifted stroke is basically preferable to one that is sliced.

I have inserted the word 'slightly' for reasons which become apparent in the chapter on spin.

I have used 'basically' because there are many occasions when it is necessary or desirable deliberately to slice the ball for strategical or tactical reasons.

Continuing this search for a swing which enables the 'racket to stay with the ball' (the American expression covering this theory) one must look down on a shot being made.

Reverting to the previous chapter to recall the law that force equals mass times acceleration, mass is impressed into strokes by rotation and forward movement of the body.

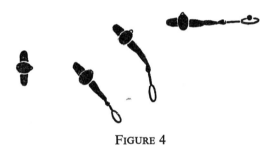

FIGURE 4

Figure 4 shows the path of the racket, viewed from above during a typical standing forehand drive. Rotation puts body weight into the shot, so adding mass and increasing racket head acceleration. Thus more force is applied to the ball than when there is no rotation of the body.

This rotation is unlikely to be so pronounced in a forehand drive made when running forwards. When running across the baseline in chase of a wide return the rotation shown in Figure 4 may be exceeded.

The drawing is not intended to show the exact relationship between racket head and shoulders; that will be covered later.

Ignoring the shoulder movement, the racket head movement,

in a powerful and near perfect—technically—drive produced by, say, Jaroslav Drobny follows roughly the path show in Figure 5 when viewed from above.

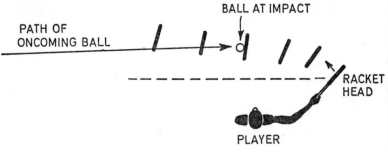

FIGURE 5

Lines drawn parallel with the path of the oncoming ball show that the racket head begins its forward travel on a line nearer to the body than the line of the oncoming ball and finishes on a line slightly beyond it.

This type of swing has a special name—the 'in-out swing'. It is the only one which allows the shoulder to move into the drive while keeping the racket strings in contact with the ball for the maximum possible time.

A little experimenting with swings should quickly convince readers that it is virtually impossible to turn the body into the shot, to impart lift, and to maximise the time of contact between ball and gut when using a swing where the racket head starts outside the line of the oncoming ball and finishes inside it—the 'out to in swing'.

Nevertheless, many players use such a swing, 90 per cent of them slicing the shot. They usually maintain fair control but only increase power by speeding the swing of the racket, a process which inevitably steepens the curve which relates safety and speed.

In addition, because of the rising flight caused by slice, there is an upper limit to the speed they can apply while keeping the ball in court.

In theory, if not quite in practice, there is no limit to speed when top spin is used.

This explanation may seem long, elaborate and at times repetitive. Yet, I believe it is important for any player bent on improving to understand all this. With this understanding he is better able to answer the basic questions which crop up sooner or later in most careers: 'Shall I base my ground strokes mainly on power or on accuracy?' and 'Are my ground strokes suited to my physique, temperament, character and, therefore, the type of game I play? Can they take me where I would wish to go without change or will they need radical alteration?'

Juniors, players who are about to embark on a serious attempt to improve, or experienced players who seem stuck in a rut can help themselves by asking themselves those questions immediately—and answering them with as much honesty as possible.

Before moving from the theory to the practice of ground strokes, let me record unequivocally that, whether a player depends on power, accuracy, or a mixture of both, I am absolutely convinced that slightly lifted drives hit with an in to out swing are far and away more reliable, effective and effort free than any other, all else being equal.

On the forehand this swing can be obtained with almost any grip but most top flight players hold their rackets in a very similar manner, using what is universally known as the 'Eastern grip'.

This is obtained by holding the racket in the left hand with its handle towards you, parallel with the ground, and with the racket face at right angles to the ground. Then the right hand should simply 'shake hands' with the handle.

As an additional safeguard, the right hand can be spread flat against the strings and then slid back along the handle before closing around it near the end.

Just as every individual has his own handshake, so each player will have his own, minute variations of the Eastern grip. These do not matter; in fact, it is not absolutely essential to use this grip at all. But when no strong preference is felt for another and no physical reason against using it exists, it is the grip which is likeliest to prove the most successful.

Now, hitting a tennis ball is a physical act which produces feelings in the body rather than thoughts in the mind.

The feeling of a forehand drive hit with a true Eastern grip is one of the racket being an extension of the arm and the racket face the palm of the hand. The impact is as though one has slapped the ball back again with the absolute middle of the palm.

However, because of individual variations, this part of the palm may be either slightly under or over the rear flat of the racket handle. In such cases, the racket may feel slightly less an extension of the arm and slightly more a separate instrument. Be quite clear that in making ground strokes the racket is swung at the ball as distinct from thrown or punched. This

---

The important thing to bear in mind when considering the production of all strokes is that the racket can only act on the ball so long as it remains in contact with it.

This means that the elasticity of the gut and ball must be taken into account but, more important, so must the horizontal line travelled by the racket head during the time the strings are actually working on the ball.

Thus, to obtain 'weight of stroke' (this means the ball feels 'heavy' when the opponent tries to return it) the racket head must travel along the same horizontal line as the ball itself and that line should be straight from the point where the ball is struck to the target spot at the other end of the court, i.e. a flat, no-spin drive.

The loss in power when top spin or chop is imparted is proportional to the cosine of the angle made by the path taken by the racket head and the court surface (the horizontal).

In tennis language, to put penetration ('weight of shot') into strokes a player must make his racket 'stay with the ball'. This feature is particularly noticeable in the ground strokes of Donald Budge. Penetration should not be confused with speed through the air when this speed is not related to the angle the ball makes with the court; in plane geometry the shortest distance between two points is a straight line.

The following three sets of sequence drawings represent champions serving, hitting a back-hand drive under severe pressure and hitting a fore-hand drive from behind the base line.

All three sequences are conglomerates and are fine examples of the basics of tennis made under the tensions of top class championship play. Because I believe that individuals should use their own eyes in order to discover styles suitable to themselves I am deliberately not interpreting the drawings. They serve as bases for understanding how good orthodox strokes should be produced but there is still ample room for individuality.

After studying these drawings endeavour to watch players in action, either in person or on television. Valuable as static figures may be, tennis is a moving game which can best be learnt by studying movement.

theory is dealt with fully in the chapter on service. For the moment remember 'swing at the ball for ground strokes'.

This, I feel, is momentarily as far as one can go in a book. It is now necessary for the reader to revise the last two chapters and then go on to a court to experiment; to see where his fore-hand drive fits in with general theory.

If he is a beginner, how best to begin? Now that televised tennis is so widespread, I recommend two or three sessions of watching the top players, to get the general idea, then a few tries on the court, preferably with a friend who can either keep the ball going or who will be patient enough to throw succes-sions of balls for hitting. Follow this with another look at the stars, another attempt or two, and then take one or two lessons with one of the professionals on the L.T.A. register. The list is obtainable from: The Secretary, Lawn Tennis Association, Barons Court, London W.14.

He will endeavour to mould your natural tendencies into shots that will fulfil the requirements of the top class of play to which you aspire.

5

Spin

Though spin is seldom used today in the deliberate way it was in the early 1900's and immediately after the first world war, most tournament players use spin to a greater or lesser degree.

Spin, so far as ground strokes are concerned, may be divided into three types, top spin, chop or under spin and slice.

Top Spin

Top spin makes the top of the ball revolve longitudinally in the same direction as its line of flight (see Fig. 6).

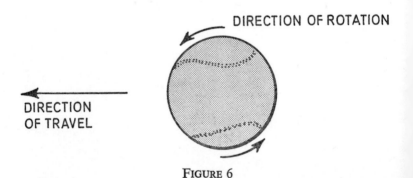

FIGURE 6

Providing there is a little nap on the ball, the rotation of the ball will increase wind resistance at its top, reduce it at its bottom. Following the line of least resistance, the ball will dip in flight.

When the ball pitches, however, the rotation lessens ground resistance, so causing the ball to bound high and forward.

Top spin can be applied heavily by brushing the racket strings up and over the ball. It can be applied less heavily by lifting the ball slightly, the racket turning slightly over during its travel (see Fig. 7).

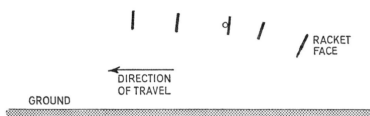

RACKET FACE

DIRECTION OF TRAVEL

GROUND

FIGURE 7

Figure 7 shows the slight lift and turn of the racket face during a 'lifted' drive. This is why lift and top spin are often interchanged in use.

Chop or Under Spin

Chop or under spin is the reverse of top spin, the ball being struck from top to bottom and rotated longitudinally so that the bottom of the ball rotates towards the line of flight (see Fig. 8).

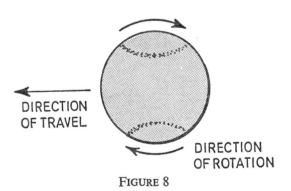

DIRECTION OF TRAVEL

DIRECTION OF ROTATION

FIGURE 8

Chop or under spin increases wind resistance to the bottom of the ball, reduces it at the top. The ball, following the line of

43

least resistance, rises in its flight. But when it pitches the rotation increases ground resistance and so the ball tends to skid through low and hold back.

Slice

Slice is a mixture of chop, which causes a longitudinal backwards rotation, and of side spin (see Fig. 9).

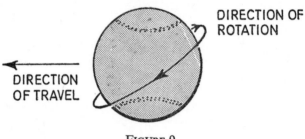

DIRECTION OF
ROTATION

DIRECTION
OF TRAVEL

FIGURE 9

The tendency of the ball is to rise in the air, and to keep low when it bounces. Whether its rise exceeds that of a chop or its bound remains lower depends on a variety of factors including the surface of the court, the nap on the ball, and the confidence of the striker. Generally, the chop is executed more purposefully, powerfully and confidently than the slice, so the ball travels more directly and lies well down after pitching. A tentative safety-first slice floats the ball through the air and lifts it after pitching. It is easy meat to any agile and ambitious volleyer.

There are, in play, two types of slice, one tentative where the racket digs at the ball and scoops it up, the other where the racket, though it imparts slice, travels very firmly and definitely straight through the point in the air where it makes contact with the ball.

In back court rally play this can be a very aggressive stroke, but it remains less useful than top spin for evading or embarrassing an opponent who volleys strongly and continually.

At park, club or even minor county levels of tennis, spin can be devastatingly effective. In top class play this is less so, for spin can only be applied at the expense of speed and speed allied to placement is the main weapon of practically every champion.

Perhaps speed should be defined in this context: it means the time a ball takes to travel from the racket to the target spot on the opponent's court.

Now use of top spin allows the ball to be hit at a terrific speed through the air but because of top spin makes the ball dip violently, it has to be given a far higher trajectory drive than a flat drive when the target is beyond the service line.

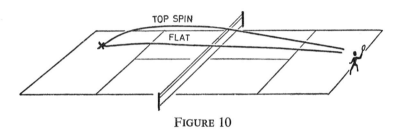

FIGURE 10

Figure 10 shows the relative path of a flat and top spin drive from the racket head to a point X in the backhand corner. The top spin drive clearly sends the ball on a much longer path and will need to be hit very much harder than the flat shot if it is to take a shorter time to reach X.

With chop or slice the effect is even worse, for the spin makes the ball rise during flight and so it must be hit softer if it is not to go beyond the target spot.

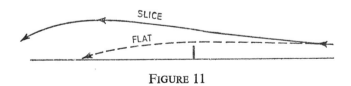

FIGURE 11

Figure 11 shows how two shots hit at a similar height with a similar speed, one with slice or chop, the other without spin (flat) will cause the ball to travel through the air.

45

There is one situation in which top spin is extremely valuable and that is when the opponent is attacking near the net. Then a heavily spun, speedy shot will dip viciously beyond his racket —or force him to volley upwards and defensively—if he reaches the ball. The main loss of speed relative to the ground will not matter because it will occur after the ball has passed the volleyer; the ball will still be travelling too quickly for him to turn, chase and catch it up.

In addition, the shorter ground distance—not air distance— between the hit and pitch of a top spin drive relative to a flat drive enables the striker to use far acuter angles.

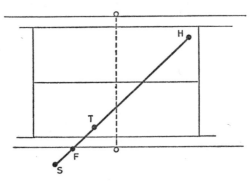

FIGURE 12

Figure 12 shows the relative air flight of three balls hit from point H with the same strength, one with top spin, another flat, the third with slice. The dip caused by top spin will cause the ball to pitch at point T while the flat shot will not pitch till F—outside the court. S pitches even farther out.

This is valuable both defensively when meeting a volleyer and offensively when forcing an opponent well beyond the sideline prior to a deep drive to the opposite corner.

This technique is exploited particularly well by Rod Laver and Manuel Santana in men's and Darlene Hard and Lesley Turner in women's tennis.

However, it can be seen that spin is used here in a positional or manœuvring sense. Providing he can reach the ball in fair comfort, the spin itself will scarcely embarrass the opponent.

46

This is not so in lower grades of tennis. I have yet to meet the ordinary park player who is not worried by chop, while top spin can, and frequently does, force average players to hit so carefully that all sting goes from their games.

An additional use of top spin is control, an important factor in those grades of tennis where new balls are scarce. At Wimbledon, where the balls are changed after the 7th, 16th, 25th, 34th and so on games, there is scarcely time for the nap to be destroyed. But a few sets on a public asphalt court reduce even the finest ball to marble smoothness and, with wind resistance so reduced, top spin is essential if the ball is not to fly.

It is also useful on courts where the baseline is near the backstop; I well recall as an inexperienced junior being completely baffled by a man who hit a succession of heavily topped, semi-lobs which pitched near the baseline and had me spending most of the morning entangled in the all too near stop netting.

Such shots must be countered when the ball is rising but it requires quite a high standard of skill to take the ball consistently on the rise and move it around the court enough to create openings or break up the opponent.

But be reminded that in top class play spin is very subservient to speed and accuracy. Not since 1930, when Tilden last won, has a Wimbledon singles champion profited from extensive and deliberate use of intentional spin.

Not that the current champions hit the ball completely flat. All use spin to some degree, that degree being the point where the speed of the flat drive is given just that modicum of lift—'lift' is the modern word for slight top spin—to keep the ball under commercial control. Perhaps Pancho Segura, whom many readers will have seen either live or on television, is the finest exemplar of the lifted forehand drive even though he uses both hands to make the shot.

For winning tennis, then, at park or club level do not be afraid to experiment with spin as a means of forcing errors from the opponent. At higher levels keep spin very much in its place as a servant to be used for opening up the opponent's court or beating a volleyer. Remember, too, that the best ground shots in the world are only about 60 per cent effective in top class play. They must be supported by equally good serving accuracy and power and naturally aggressive, enterprising and punishing volleying before they can take a man to the top.

Beware of slicing off the backhand. It is such an easy shot to develop and, once developed, is as difficult to cure as dope addiction. And a sliced backhand is the easiest target in the world for an adequate and nimble volleyer.

On the forehand the easy habit to acquire is top spin. This is far less dangerous than slice on the backhand.

Unless a player has a very fixed and reasonable determination to reach the very highest levels, he would be ill advised to allow a friend or coach to persuade him to change. Since Vic Seixas, who won Wimbledon in 1953, used excessive top on nearly every forehand, I am almost inclined to say never change a strong forehand which uses top spin for a flatter drive simply to be more orthodox. Certainly weigh the pros and cons very carefully, indeed a dozen times over—and then another dozen. But beware of changes.

Service sequence

Forehand sequence

Backhand sequence

Tony Roche

Ann Haydon Jones

Margaret Court

(*Below*) J. E. Lundquist

bove) John Newcombe

Rod Laver

Billie-Jean King

6

Service, Use of Service and Return of Service

Earlier I suggested that tennis strokes are physical activities which one 'feels' in the arms, body, legs and stomach. They are not intellectual phenomena, although intellect fulfils an important role when strokes are being learnt or modified.

The Registered Professionals tried some years ago to translate those feelings into words. They said:

(1) In making ground strokes you should SWING your racket at the ball.

(2) In serving, the racket head should be THROWN at the ball.

(3) When volleying, make your racket PUNCH the ball.

To repeat, swing for ground strokes, throw for service and punch when volleying. Those are the feelings which must be sought, the racket-moving techniques which must be learnt through thoughtful application and 'grooved' by constant, machine-like repetition.

There are several ways of learning but these four are probably the most important:

(1) By listening to verbal instructions.

(2) By reading.

(3) By viewing demonstrations or pictorial instructions.

(4) By inductive reasoning.

In fact most young people appear to respond best to (3), visual instruction, though the other methods will all add their contributions to the final outcome of knowledge or performance.

For this reason I very strongly recommend that any serious reader makes an all-out effort quickly to see the three training films I produced under the joint sponsorship of the Nestlé Sports Foundation and Slazengers. Lawn tennis is dynamic and active, not static, so that visual instruction, especially at beginner and intermediate stages, should first be moving. Once the basic ideas are understood, ordinary sequence pictures provide ideal evidence for closer study, especially of the finer points of stroke play. And it is these finer points which so often differentiate the great player from the good or moderate performers who are seeking higher honours.

The Nestlé-Slazenger films are on 16 mm. black and white stock with an optical sound track and details of distribution are available from the Nestlé Sports Foundation, St. George's House, Croydon, Surrey.

It may seem a trifle odd that the recommendation to study films has been delayed to a chapter headed service, but that is because the service is an unnatural shot to the great majority of people who take up lawn tennis.

FIGURE 13

It is also one of the most valuable and important, as anyone who has seen play at Wimbledon or Wembley, either at first hand or via television, knows all too well.

There is throughout the world a widespread belief that 'what comes naturally' must be best. This is a fair way from the truth so far as tennis is concerned, especially in serving.

Give an average man (or woman) a tennis racket and ball, take him on a court and ask him to serve. The odds are heavily in favour of his throwing the ball up and hitting it as though hammering a nail into the wall (see Fig. 13).

The V formed by the thumb and first finger will be in the middle of the back, flat part of the racket handle with the knuckles of the fingers pointing towards the spot where the server is aiming.

The only throwing action this resembles is that of an expert darts player. There can be no question of wrist snap either snapping the racket head into the rapid acceleration which converts a fast service into an untouchable cannon-ball or spinning the ball so viciously that it discomfits the receiver with its break and kick.

If the man has seen top class play then there is a good chance that he will attempt the full swing of the stars, but still with the grip just described; it is known by professional coaches as the frying-pan grip and from here on I shall abbreviate this to FPG.

Now it is probable that most readers of this book will have advanced beyond the FPG stage of tennis. Yet, without knowing it, there is a strong likelihood that its influence is still being suffered and this will survive until obliterated by fresh grooving.

Let me make it quite clear why the FPG or, when the hand moves clockwise round the handle, the eastern grip as used for the forehand, is unsuited to service.

Service is the one stroke in the game on which the opponent need have no effect. One stands with ball in one hand, racket in the other at the exact position of choice. There is no need to hurry and one can survey the position at leisure.

This unique opportunity is too precious to be wasted. One

must seek to put the opponent at the worst possible disadvantage by shrewd use of the four varieties of attack:

(1) Power.

(2) Spin.

(3) Placement and control.

(4) Variation.

Taking power first, it is the child of force and from Newton's second law of motion we know this to be equal to mass times acceleration. In serving, this acceleration relates to the speed and direction in which the racket head meets the ball.

This speed of racket head movement derives from the knees, hips, shoulders, arm swing, elbow and wrist. The wrist being related to the grip and the grip being the feature which is, perhaps, most unnatural, I shall deal with it first.

Many quite good players make no dynamic use of their wrists in serving. When it is realized that the repeated cracks of the whip heard at a circus are said to be caused by the tip of the whip breaking the sound barrier and that this is achieved by a flick of the wrist, it is simple to understand why it is a mistake to keep the wrist rigid when serving.

Try a little experiment which I conducted immediately before writing this paragraph. Put your arm on the table so that the flat front of your wrist is fully on the surface. Raise the forearm slightly and ascertain how much backward and forward wrist movement you can obtain. It will not bend back very far and forward movement is not very extensive either, 45 degrees or so just about covering the entire range of the movement.

Now try moving the wrist from side to side. There is a valuable increase in the range of movement, the arc in my case covering about 90 degrees.

Apart from any question of total movement, there is also the importance of useful movement. Take a racket and hold it in the air at the striking position of service using either the eastern or FPG. Try bending the wrist back to get snap. Then slowly bring the racket head forward without moving the arm, i.e. by using the wrist only. Almost at once the racket face is looking downwards and a ball struck in that position would go into the net.

Now swivel the racket around to the backhand grip and hold the racket so that the opposite face to the one that hits backhand drives is now looking down the court. The position may seem unnatural, but just test for the increased range of useful movement it yields.

Test for acceleration, too. Simply by using the backhand grip and snapping the wrist you will soon be able to make the strings 'swish' loudly through the air, something you will not achieve using either the eastern or FPG.

This 'swish' generated by wrist flick or whip is what converts a powerful service swing into one which regularly speeds the ball through for untouchable aces.

It is also the key factor in imparting really vicious spin to the ball, so making the service difficult to handle, instead of a slight twist that makes service return easier rather than more difficult.

However, before moving on to spin there is another aspect of the swing which must be analysed since this has important effects on pace, power and direction. The factor is the distance behind the body one can swing the arm before the break at the elbow and loop takes place.

Before attempting to learn service it is vital to watch and analyse one of the great servers in action; someone like Gonzalez, Laver, Ashe perhaps.

Having watched, you will know that as the throw up arm goes forward to toss the ball into a hitting position the other arm sweeps the racket down past the legs. The two arms work in synchronism like the blades of a pair of scissors.

The serving arm continues straight backwards for a while before the elbow closes to let the racket fall behind the back, from which position it is 'thrown' at the ball. The movement is similar to throwing in from the longfield at cricket.

Everybody has a natural position where this part of the entire action or throw begins. With some it is when the elbow is about parallel with the waist. Others carry the arm round till the elbow is almost level with the shoulders before letting it 'break'.

All other things being equal, the nearer to shoulder level one can swing the elbow, the better it is.

Figure 14 oversimplifies the entire situation but is still near

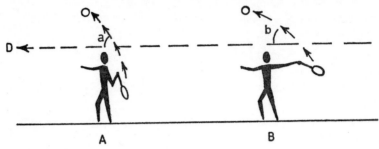

FIGURE 14

enough to accuracy to illustrate the meaning. Pinman A breaks early, the dotted line linking racket head and ball approximating to the line the racket must take. The same thing applies to pinman B. The angular difference between racket line and the direction the ball has to travel, as shown by D, is far greater for A than B.

Taking oversimplified relationships, if angle B is 45 degrees, the power generated in the direction D is proportional to the cosine of 45 degrees or 0·707 of total power.

If angle is 30 degrees, cosine 30 degrees = 0·866. Thus the server develops

$$\frac{0.866 - 0.707}{1} = \frac{\cdot159}{1}$$

i.e. 16 per cent more power.

I must again stress that this is an oversimplification, although the general theory approximates to correctness.

The other gain is in direction. Look at Figure 15. Line A is equal to the horizontal distance between the racket head and an imaginary vertical line from ball to ground. Line B refers to a similar measurement for server B.

T ━━━━ R   T ━━━━━ R

    A   B

FIGURE 15

If the throw up is x inches off true for server A the change in the direction of point R (the racket head) as it moves towards T (the throw up) will make a greater angle than a similar error in throw up for server B.

In the rough diagram the line for server B is roughly 35 per cent longer than for server A. In terms of accuracy (which means going inside or outside a given court line) this is very appreciable; certainly enough to differentiate between a formidable service and a poor one.

The third advantage of a longer pull back of the racket lies in superior cleanness and rhythm of the swing.

All these points are more complex in action than I could hope to make clear by words alone, but I believe the discerning reader will now be able to understand why a first class service is governed so much by the grip and the extent of the swing back or pull back.

A little earlier I used the words 'throw up' and 'toss' in serving. Great servers do neither; they 'place up' the ball, carrying the left hand (if they are right-handed players) high into the air, holding on to the ball as long as possible and seemingly, placing it in position to be hit.

This has a secondary function, that of keeping the left shoulder well up to the hitting position. If the left arm is allowed to drop there is a danger of the entire left side falling away from the ball long before it is struck so that no mass is imparted to the ball; and we know that force is proportional to mass times acceleration.

This can be seen in most servers simply by forgetting the ball and watching only their right legs. If the leg moves of its own volition and before the crucial last stage of the swing is in motion, the chances are strong that balance has been broken by letting part of the body fall away to the left of the ball.

The new foot-fault rule which permits jumping and swinging one leg over the baseline before the ball has been struck has changed the serving techniques of many players. Nevertheless, broadly speaking, a top-class server can deliver a very fast ball without letting either of his feet leave the ground. Anyone seeking a fearsome service should first develop a control of balance which allows him to keep both feet fixed in position while delivering. Not until this is mastered should he experiment with the jump-swing techniques used so successfully by Fred Stolle and Roger Taylor.

Where to 'place up' the ball depends on a number of factors both general and individual.

To orientate position stand for a moment with both feet on the baseline at the spot to the right of the baseline centre from which you normally serve to the first court. Probably the spot is about 12 in. to the right of the centre mark. Hold the ball as high up in the air as possible with the upper part of your left arm touching your nose.

Looking up at the ball first and then past the arm straight down the court gives the line. The points marked on the ball in Figure 16 are approximately where the centre of your racket strings should strike the ball for various types of service.

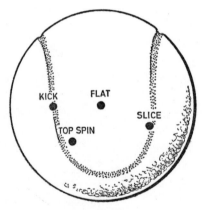

FIGURE 16

These positions will vary somewhat in accordance with the position relative to your body in which you 'place up' the ball, your height, etc.

Most top class servers stand with the line of their shoulders more or less at right angles to the line of the net. The left foot is three or so inches behind the baseline, making an angle of roughly 45 degrees to the right of a line the ball will travel when struck. The right foot is comfortably behind the right and a line drawn between the two feet indicates the direction a flat hit service will travel.

The 'place up' position for a flat service is such that, if allowed to drop, the ball would fall within a 4-in. radius of the toes of the left foot, usually.

A few servers will place up the ball more to the left, others farther to the right. The actual position depends on the individual swing and interpretation of body weight transference.

The most powerful body movement in serving is a rising spiral. Stand with your feet about 12 in. apart and let your knees bend a little while swivelling the whole body around in a clockwise direction, but keeping it upright.

Now thrust upwards with the knees, reaching up on the balls of the feet and simultaneously snapping the body back to its straight position. Make this whole upward spiralling movement as harmonious and powerful as possible. That is the action to seek when serving.

The extent of the turn and the pattern of the swing are inextricably related so no specific rule can be laid down other than that the body weight and swing should give the feeling at the moment of impact of being right behind the line of the service.

If there is any sensation of toppling to left or right something is wrong, probably in the 'place up' but perhaps in general balance.

Experiment until balance becomes as perfect as a human being may reasonably expect. Remember, it is not possible consistently to generate power from an insecure or badly balanced foundation.

The flat service goes quickest from A to B but the margin of error is far less than with the slice, kick or top spin service, irrespective of any embarrassment the spin itself causes the receiver.

The slice service is made by hitting fractionally on the outside (right) of the ball, probably just below its 'equator' in order to start the ball on a slightly more upwards flight than when serving without spin; the spin reacts with the air to pull the ball downwards once forward momentum slackens.

Slice curves the ball from the server's right to left and makes it skid somewhat after bouncing—if the slice is severe.

If the slice is not severe the curve, rather than dragging the receiver well to his, the receiver's, right, merely lines up the ball in the best spot for the receiver's forehand drive whilst popping the ball up to an easy height for 'murdering'.

A heavily sliced service delivered from a point midway between the middle of the baseline and the sideline and aimed at the sideline of the first court should force the receiver well beyond the tram-lines and leave his deep backhand corner extremely vulnerable to the next shot.

However, if such a service fails to pitch on or near the sideline and sizzle with spin, the server himself is wide open to a fast return of service to the backhand corner.

Actually, sizzle is too strong a word. Too much slice slows down the ball overmuch, too little does not make it curve. There is an optimum amount of spin which balances speed and curve. Each individual must find this by experience.

Figure 17 shows the effects. No spin lines up the ball perfectly for the receiver.

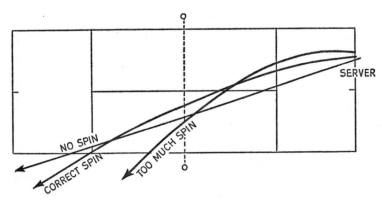

FIGURE 17

Only excessive spin at the cost of speed will make the ball follow the 'too much spin' line and this presents the receiver with ample time and infinite angles for his return.

Correct spin strikes the right balance.

58

Note that the three lines start from slightly different spots. These indicate that the greater the spin, the more to the right of the ball one must hit. To compensate for direction, one must also therefore 'place up' the ball more to the right.

The slice service is used mostly in the first court as shown but it can be directed towards the centre line, so swinging the ball into the receiver's body. Many players are ill at ease returning shots that swing into them.

The slice can also be used in the second court either to drag the receiver to the middle of his baseline or, by aiming at the sideline, to swing the ball into his body. The middle line slice service in this court can be very useful in doubles play.

Returning to Figure 16, the positions for hitting the ball when delivering a kick or top spin are shown. Both these serves bear the generic title American twist, though when Maurice McLoughlin first made such services famous, this referred to the kicker.

To impart either spin the racket strings must brush the ball from left to right. This necessitates bending backwards and 'placing up' the ball both more to the left and farther backwards. Snapping the back straight and brushing the ball by using a sharp flick of the wrist modifies the follow through of the service swing.

In the flat and slice services the racket sweeps down, passing the left side of the left leg.

In the kick service it flicks out sideways to the right of the right leg, which if the back straightening is sufficiently vigorous will come forward and up almost as if stepping on to a chair.

The kick and break are caused by lateral spin. In the top-spin service there is also some forward spin caused by the racket brushing upwards and through the ball much more diagonally than in the kick.

This diagonal, as distinct from lateral, spin causes the ball to bound forward on bouncing, reducing the break and also the abruptness of the kick.

Such spins tend to swerve the ball from the server's left to his right and to make the ball break in the same direction. That is across to the backhand of a right-handed receiver. If the break and kick are both severe and the ball is delivered to the sideline this can be a very difficult service to handle. If the kick and break are not severe—and they won't be unless the back and wrist actions are vigorous—the service causes little or no difficulty. Indeed, if the receiver is quick-witted and fleet-footed, he will be able to skip round and pulverise the ball with his forehand drive.

Given speed and control, however, the server can do great damage, not only by attacking the backhand but also by serving to the forehand and kicking the ball into the receiver's body.

Apart from the techniques of serving, one must also master the psychology. Two important facets of this are variety and length.

Any one service, be it fast or spun, loses all its terrors through constant repetition. Variety keeps the receiver guessing, but beware of variety falling into regular patterns. Fast, slice, kick repeated in never changing sequence is no more varied than continuous fast serving. One's aim must be to outguess the receiver and in this context I have never seen anything smarter than Juan Couder's service when he reached match-point against Neale Fraser in the 1962 Italian Championships. For almost $4\frac{1}{2}$ hours Couder had served around medium pace and remained on the baseline.

At match-point he drooped over a snail's pace delivery and rushed to the net behind it. Utterly surprised by the change Fraser returned the ball tamely in the middle of the net.

Jaroslav Drobny used almost the same gambit when he reached match-point against Ken Rosewall in the 1954 Wimbledon final, with identical results.

Length is vital, so vital that it is almost worth serving occasional double faults in seeking to pitch the ball right up to the line. A long service, though soft, carries a reasonable degree of immunity from attack. A very fast service that pitches 4 or 5 ft. short of the service line merely feeds the receiver with pace to turn to his own advantage.

Overpressing is a common cause of faulting. The point is crucial and the server is anxious to force. So he does not 'place up' the ball high enough or he rushes the first part of the service so that the racket head is losing speed instead of accelerating when it hits the ball.

Another frequent cause of error is in hurrying the body action so that all the weight has gone through and height been lost before the ball has actually been struck.

The antidote to all this is time and relaxation. No matter what the point, whether love all in the first game or match-point to the opponent, take ample time in settling into position, survey the court thoroughly, think consciously of a slow start to the swing. Reaching to full height for the 'place up' relax the grip and wrist slightly and remember to swing. Let the racket do the work rather than forcing with the arm. If necessary bounce the ball two or three times before starting, though this should not become an automatic part of the entire serving technique.

Take two or three really deep breaths. Then, when completely composed in mind and body, wind up slowly and throw the racket head at the ball.

Whether or not to go all out for an ace is a matter of personal choice. Professionals like Gonzalez and Rosewall have developed uncanny abilities to 'play the percentages'. That is, use the shot, shots or tactics which offer the best chance of winning any particular point. One cannot generalise but, by and large, it is a better 'percentage play' on critical points to make sure of getting in a deep, well-placed, three-quarter pace delivery to the opponent's weakness as a prelude to an attack than to take a chance on an ace.

Even if your second service is very little inferior to your first, the receiver will subconsciously think it is. So when the attempted ace ends up a fault, he will move in slightly, confident that he will be able to force the pace off your second ball. And in tennis, having confidence is half-way to success in situations of this nature.

On the other hand, he will receive your first service in a more defensive state of mind and will be unlikely to attack even a moderate delivery—providing you have been varying your service speeds, spins and patterns throughout the match. If he knows beforehand what is going to happen you are in imminent danger of losing the point.

Nowadays on fast courts service is almost always followed to the net. In doing this avoid the common fault of serving, running a couple of paces and then pausing momentarily to see if it will be a fault. Each foot that one gets nearer to the net for the volley lessens the danger of being passed, increases the angles offered to the volleyer and usually enables the ball to be taken higher in the air.

So concentrate on putting in a strong, deep serve and run right in behind it without any thought of fault in your mind. The technical advantages alone will more than compensate for the occasional longer walks back following services which are faults and there is an even more important psychological advantage.

In closing right in, one builds up one's own feeling of aggression and confidence while having the reverse effect on the receiver.

Jean Borotra was the archpriest of this. Viewed dispassionately, his service was not outstanding. Yet he closed in so fast behind it and was so severe on any returns which were at all loose that the continually mounting pressure repeatedly broke down the finest returners of service of his day. And, remember, that was in the days when top class players really possessed strong ground strokes.

The corollary to a service, if it is not a fault, is return of service. Here I am reminded of a chant used by the late Wilfred Austin, father of Bunny Austin, who was a hero of Britain's Davis Cup heyday in the 1930's.

Whenever Bunny—or I, for he coached me too—returned a ball into the net, he chanted in an infuriating monotone: 'The main and primary object of the game of lawn tennis is to hit the ball over the net.'

Four or five repeats of that were so aggravating that Bunny and I moved heaven and earth to obviate any further encores. The net result so far as Bunny was concerned was that he became one of the finest returners of service the game has ever known, ranking with Rosewall, Lacoste and Kramer in that respect.

Any return of service that goes into the net or flies yards out of court must be inferior to one that limps its way back, no matter how softly. So the first object must be to return the ball. The second, to prevent the server's ensuing shot from being too aggressive. The third, to put the server in difficulties, the fourth to win the point outright.

The weaker the service, the more one can concentrate on the third and fourth objects; a missed return going for an outright winner can be compensated for on the next point. When every service is a potential ace, there is always the danger one will not even touch the ball for the next point or two so one cannot normally take too many chances, when the occasional easier delivery comes over.

This type of choice is reasonably easy to work out and experience soon tells thinking players how to decide.

The choice is more difficult when the server is also a strong volleyer. Should one get the ball back somehow, hoping he will miss the volley, or keep taking 'neck or nothing', 'against the percentages' swipes in the hope of stringing enough together to force an occasional break?

One's temperament, build, style of play and other factors must have an effect here. A persistent, small man who is fast on his feet can always hope that the ensuing volley will be less severe than the first volley and so make sure of getting the ball in play.

A more powerful but also more cumbersome man will, perhaps, be even more vulnerable to the volley than he is to the service. So his returns, perforce, will have to be more aggressive and purposeful.

Certainly, no matter how fine the limits imposed by the strength of the service, vary the returns as much as possible. Don't despise the lob, even if only as a means of causing the server to hesitate in his runs to the net.

Four games of lobs may well open up the way for a fifth game in which the returns can be effectively dinked back at his hesitant feet while he half waits for more lobs.

Vary the position in which you wait for service. Try moving 4 or 5 yds. behind the baseline—or 4 or 5 ft. inside it. Even consider using a slacker racket for receiving than when serving.

Both Arthur Ashe and Dennis Ralston use this ploy repeatedly.

Any move you can make or tactic you can adopt which makes your opponent think consciously about his service action is likely to disrupt his automatic grooving.

Such moves must be fair. Gamesmanship belittles the player who resorts to it—and ultimately impedes advancement.

Reduce the length of your swing and be content sometimes to block the ball back; if the service is fast even a blocked return will carry sufficient speed to worry the server.

Keep mentally alert because in this way it is often possible to discover clues which tell where the ball is going before it is actually struck. The opponent's throw up is sometimes a good clue to this.

As in serving, returning service successfully depends on technical skill, analytical ability, initiative and imagination. Making the utmost use of whatever abilities are possessed in these factors is the route to success. To call these into operation demands practised, applied concentration but that is vital for all shots.

It also necessitates plenty of practice, preferably with someone who serves well but who is not necessarily ambitious to become a champion.

Ideally this practice partner will serve only to aid the receiver's practice. This means sometimes feeding successions of weak services which can be hit for winners. At other times the receiver must handle kicking services, slices and sheer speed.

For the latter get the server to deliver from a yard or even two yards inside the baseline. This will obviously leave the receiver less time. Less obviously perhaps, it will offer the server wider angles. Even a moderate server can become formidable like this, which is fine for receiving practice but not quite so good for serving practice.

However, if two keen players take it turn and turn about to give each other receiving practice, the good should counter any possible harm to the service.

7

Volleying

Ground strokes are basic to tennis. One can dominate each alternate game with strong and varied serving. There are still many other shots that any aspirant to fame must acquire and of these none is more important than the volley.

Volleying returns from near the net before the ball has the chance to bounce imposes heavy pressure on the opponent. The time lag between his shots is very nearly halved irrespective of any increase in angle made possible by taking the ball nearer to the net.

The basic feel of volleying is punching or stabbing. The racket has to jab forward to meet the ball—there should be no question of the ball coming to the racket—and to ensure this, the long swing back of ground-stroke play has to be eliminated.

In ground stroke rallies one can sometimes temporise. There is no time for indecision or shilly-shallying when at the net.

The approach should be made with only one idea in mind, immediate winning of the point. The volleyer must strive to end the rally at once. If the baseliner can reach the volley with any kind of ease he should be in an advantageous position to score with a passing shot.

I should, perhaps, make it clear that this assumes the two men to be moderate players of similar standards. If one is far stronger than the other, he will be able to go to the net and volley any way he likes without running undue risk of being passed.

In tournament and match play it is not possible to end all rallies with first volleys; defenders have become adept in dinking over soft angled returns that force weak volleys and open the court for a following passing shot.

This demands that players learn low volleys—that is, volleys played below the level of the net band—as well as the easier ones that are made when the return is above waist height.

This entails two generalisations which hold true in an overwhelming preponderance of situations. The first is that depth is a volleyer's best friend. The second is that few baseliners hit with as much accuracy, power and consistency when made to play their shots after turning to regain position as they do when running uninterruptedly from side to side.

In this context there is no better 'offensive defence' for a serve-run-in-and-volley attack than a serve to the backhand followed by a deep, forceful volley deep into the backhand corner.

For every successful passing shot he produces against this gambit the average baseliner will yield two or three points on errors and a further three or four to second volleys made by the volleyer. This contrasts favourably with the more usual 'serve to one side, volley to the other' used by inexperienced or unthinking players.

To recap quickly, the first four tenets of profitable volleying are:

(1) Watch the ball carefully before meeting it with a shortened swing back, jab or punch.
(2) Punch the ball deep to the baseline.
(3) When in doubt, force the baseliner to turn when making his stroke.
(4) Think always of ending the point immediately.

To these must be added others which are, perhaps, slightly more detailed and technical.

Continuing without numbering, the next is to close right in to the net when volleying and to scorn the lob. Experience will develop judgment over this but, in general, more points are lost because the volleyer was not near enough to the net to angle the return out of reach than are ever surrendered to lobs which leave the volleyer flat-footed too near the net.

It should go without saying that the man who volleys from

within 4 ft. of the net must react more quickly and run backwards faster than one who remains 4 yds. away from the net.

Yet the alertness which is generated by audaciousness possesses its own compensation and it is surprising how soon one learns to get back to kill lobs from the advanced 'nose over the net' position.

Footwork is often neglected in volleying yet it is almost more important than in ground-stroke play. True, there are many fast rallies in which the man at the net literally has no time to move his feet.

He must, repeat must, turn and sway his body to compensate for this.

Similarly, the way the racket is held between points must show cognisance of the speed factor. In my view the racket should be held higher than in ground-stroke play so that the volleyer has only to move it sideways and forwards.

There is literally no time to bring the racket up from the usual, unthinking position before jabbing the racket to meet the ball. All too often the ball comes on to the racket before the jab or punch has started. So keep the racket positioned high to eliminate all preliminary movements.

The actual grips used depend on the individual. Most volleyers use the same grip for backhand volleys as for backhand ground strokes.

This is not necessarily so on the forehand. Given time, I suppose, most of those who use the Eastern or 'shake hands' forehand ground-stroke grip try to use it also for forehand volleys. In sharp volleying exchanges, however, many use the continental (i.e. backhand) grip for all volleys, hitting the ball with one face of the racket for the backhand, the reverse face for the forehand.

This grip is very flexible and is well adapted for the use of spin. It is also a slightly more sensitive grip so that one 'feels' the ball on the forehand side more than with the Eastern grip. This is important when making drop volleys or when volleying returns a few inches off the ground. Such low volleys demand the use of a little controlling backspin if the ball is to be kept within the confines of the court.

Volleying should be learnt from the first lesson onwards, whether that lesson be given by a highly skilled professional or a well-meaning, kindly but not particularly knowledgeable friend.

Have the friend throw a succession of balls which can be jabbed with a shortened swing, punch shot which begins just above the height at which the ball will be met and finishes just below that height.

Just as the backswing should be shortened, so should the follow through.

The wrist must be firmly braced at the moment of impact, which should be slightly in advance in time, and therefore distance, of the striking point for ground strokes.

Volley exchanges are usually speedy, which necessitates watching the ball carefully. This entails keeping the eyes nearer to the ball than in ground-stroke play, a factor covered by slight crouching and, on low volleys, by bending the knees and sinking right down to the ball.

Many players fail to continue their forward runs after making first volleys. This is wrong because volley play is always fluid and the volleyer must keep moving, preferably forwards.

This is not a particularly natural thing to do so it must be acquired through purposeful practice. Two against one using a couple of dozen or more balls is ideal for this. The two on the baseline should hold as many balls as possible in their hands, firing a fresh one without hesitation the split second the one in flight goes into the net or out of reach. This form of rallying should be so fast that the volleyer literally has no time to pause or think.

If two practice opponents are not available, the aspirant to fame must make do with one. I can assure readers from personal experience that a really keen friend can keep one hopping around the net pretty fast.

Two players can also practise by volleying to one another from positions inside the service court. This I feel to be slightly dangerous. Most readers will possess a rough knowledge of Pavlov's famous conditioning experiments with dogs. This applies equally to humans so that two men who over-practise volleying a ball back and forth are likely to find themselves volleying to their opponents rather than into the gaps when they come to play matches.

The aim of practice is 'grooving' and in volleying the grooving should be to put the ball way beyond the opponent's reach.

By all means indulge in a little to and fro volleying to get the feel of the ball but revert very quickly to some form of practice which sends the ball to far-off corners.

If the partner is hitting from the baseline, put boxes in the corners and try to hit them with your volleys. If speedier practice is needed, play goals. Form goals on each service-line by putting a box or racket a yard or so inside each sideline.

Then try to volley wide of one another and between these 'makeshift goal-posts', the first one to score, say ten goals, winning the match.

Practise against a wall, starting from 10 or 12 ft. away and moving forward after each volley until you are only 3 or 4 ft. away from the wall. Work hard at this to develop both control of the ball and speed of racket handling. Frank Sedgman learnt to volley this way.

Continuous practice, apart from 'grooving' one's volleys, also increases one's speed of reaction and racket handling. There is an upper limit to the speed at which one can react, overcome the mechanical inertia of the racket and move. However, as nerve messages can travel at 130 miles per second, the time taken by the brain giving an arm muscle an instruction is scarcely likely to prevent one from getting a racket in the way of even a full-blooded smash from only 2 or 3 yds. away.

Indeed, those who saw Ken Rosewall beat Tony Trabert in the semi-finals of the 1954 Wimbledon singles still talk of the two Trabert smashes which he volleyed for winners though only 6 ft. or so away from the crunch of impact. I still recall Peter Wilson's phrase in his *Daily Mirror* report—'This wasn't anticipation, it was thought reading.'

Rosewall was not one of the most instinctive volleyers in the game but by sheer practice he became one of the best, thus providing a reminder that where there is the will—and the enjoyment—there is undoubtedly the way.

69

In present-day men's tennis it is now taken for granted that the server always runs in behind each service, directing that service either down the centre line or to the opponent's weakness, the choice depending on his individual ideas about tennis.

Two caveats must be made: one is to avoid becoming stereotyped; 'keep the opponent guessing' is one of the few 'absolutes' of tennis.

The other is to become equally happy volleying balls that come from any and all directions. Many—probably most—players, even up to Drobny's standard, feel happier volleying shots from one direction than from others. In Drobny's case, this direction is usually from a right-handed player's backhand; when the ball comes from the other wing they feel awkward.

This totally unnecessary limitation of effectiveness should never be allowed to develop. In fact, it won't if one takes as much trouble to volley against forehand drives as against backhands.

Indeed, once one has reached a standard that yields a little leeway, it is a good exercise in self-discipline as well as good practice and good fun to play occasional weak opponents by attacking only the forehand side.

One serves only once in every two games so it is necessary to break the opponent's service to win sets and matches. This entails going to the net behind ground strokes. Where should these be placed?

Apart from the obvious 'deep to the weakness', there are other general principles, the chief of which is to make the opponent run diagonally backwards whenever possible.

Think for a moment. You have played a cross-court forehand drive which pitches near the junction of the service and side-lines, taking the opponent into his forehand tram-lines.

If your next shot is deep to the backhand corner, he must run across the court and away from the net.

Unless his peripheral vision sweeps about 270 degrees he will not be able to keep his eyes on the ball and also see you or your feet.

He must guess your position and as not one player in a hundred imagines opposition positions, you have an ideal chance to go in for a winning volley.

The opposite of this gambit is a drive deep to the baseline followed by a shot which pitches on the centre service-line and keeps low. This forces the opponent to hurry forward to dig up the ball from a position which severely limits his angles. A volleyer with fast reflexes can literally blanket the net in this way. Indeed, those were the tactics Mervyn Rose used to beat the defending champion Dick Savitt at Wimbledon in 1952—and Savitt possessed probably the finest ground and passing strokes of any post-World War Two player.

There are two philosophies in net play behind ground strokes and a would-be champion should be proficient in both.

The first—and most common—posits waiting for a short return from the opponent, swooping on to it and continuing the run to the net, irrespective of the goodness or badness of the approach shot. Thus the opponent's return must be an unknown quantity and one's volley may turn out to be either a formality or a headlong dive at a flashing passing shot.

In fact, one learns to execute deep, powerful approach shots off the weak returns and these generally force weak responses which are simple to volley out of reach. The weak response is not guaranteed.

The other philosophy is to rally from back court until one spots a weak return leaving the opponent's racket. One then rushes forward to take that weak return on the fly.

Inevitably, it is seldom possible to play such volleys from as near to the net as when swooping in behind an approach shot made off a short return.

The best way of volleying these floating, weak returns is to use one's normal ground-stroke swing. This is known technically as a volley drive and I know of only one English coach who teaches this shot. It is said to be risky and when attempted without confidence it probably is. Taken boldly and with the intention of forcing the opponent to run wide at top speed, the volley drive off a 'floating' return is a devastating weapon which tears at the opponent's stamina leaving him considerably weakened by the end of a well-contested match.

This, like all forms of volleying, tends to build up a cumulative effect over any match. It is comparatively simple to remain calm and evade the net-rusher's racket at love all in the first set.

Later on, when hot and a little tired, and when the net rusher has begun to know one's pet shots and habits, the gaps can look very, very small.

That is why many volleyers win matches when their losing volleys exceed their winners. The balance exceed their winners. The balance comes from mistakes made by the baseliner in attempting passing shots.

The classic case of this occurred at Wimbledon shortly after the war. M. D. Deloford, beaten by A. G. Roberts in the first round of the Championship singles, found himself again in opposition to Roberts in the All England Plate, an event open to those beaten in the first and second round of the Championship singles proper.

Having lost from baseline, Deloford decided to rush the net on everything. In three sets he volleyed the ball only twice, each time for an error. Yet he won the match, his net rushings forcing more errors than successful passing shots from Roberts.

This may be an extreme case yet it emphasizes the pressure volleying puts on an opponent. That is why volleying must be learnt concurrently with ground strokes.

And this holds true whether the ambition be to win Wimbledon or the local club singles.

A sweeping assertion? Not when one holds a strong belief that playing tennis should be exciting and fun.

8

Chess-board Tennis

One very effective method of building up a net attack is shown in Figure 18. It arises quite naturally from the dozens of returns which float down the middle of the court in every match played.

The hitter plays his shot along line S1, preferably with top spin, forcing the receiver to move towards the net and beyond his forehand sideline to X1. Sometimes his return will be too strong to permit the second shot A2 deep to his backhand corner.

Frequently it will not, and so the hitter will be able to aim for the deep backhand corner and move in to position HN where his comfortable net coverage is shown by a line.

Ignoring a lob, only the shaded portions of the court are open to the receiver from X2.

But trace his path from X1 to X2. It is diagonally backwards, so he will be quite unable to watch the ball and the area P2 available to a cross-court return. Additionally, few players below top class are capable of really good control on the backhand when running backwards and even fewer possess a fast and reliable backhand drive straight down the sideline. In this situation it has to be very accurate as the path of the ball is slightly towards the volleyer; the cross-court return runs away from him.

Providing the cross-court drive S1 is severe and near to the sideline—say 3 to 6 in.—this sequence will win seven points out of ten once it is mastered.

On the other hand, if the cross-court opener S1 is not severe or well placed, the superior position in the rally is passed to receiver.

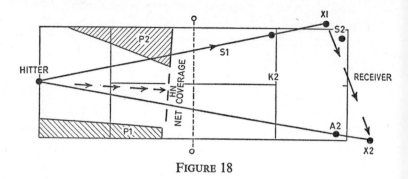

FIGURE 18

For that reason S1 is generally more effective when the receiver plays the ball from a spot nearer to his forehand sideline than the one shown in Figure 18.

It is also an effective gambit when the opening shot to the spot near to the junction of the side and service lines is a severe backhand slice which causes the ball to skid and keep low.

As a final means of harassing the receiver, instead of hitting the second shot to A2 every time, every fourth, fifth or sixth time the sequence is used the second shot should be hit to S2.

This may be to the receiver's forehand but he will be scampering to cover A2, will have to hit the ball after turning and running behind S2 and very few players are as strong hitting 'on the turn' as they are when oscillating regularly from one side of the court to the other and back.

The sequence has been built up from a frequently recurring rally position. Thoughtful readers will already have spotted a better way of bringing it into operation—that is, when serving, especially when the server possesses a strong, swerving sliced delivery. This is one of the reasons why Jack Kramer is generally conceded to have been one of the most difficult ever servers to break.

Time and again he would bang over a service which swung fast, skidded low and forced the receiver to scrape a return back near the ground from point X1. Forehand or backhand, Kramer then forced the next return before moving in for a simple kill on the fifth shot of the rally; Kramer's third shot.

He, too, would keep the receiver on tenterhooks by slamming

occasional services straight down the middle line, the ball pitching at K2 and aceing the receiver.

A final reminder. The severity and accuracy of S1 are the keys to success in this sequence.

Figure 19 shows a typical situation in match play which costs the hitter many points which he should win.

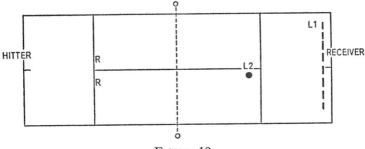

FIGURE 19

A rally develops and the hitter drives a ball which pitches somewhere along the line L1, forcing the receiver to retreat beyond the position shown in the diagram. At least half the time the receiver's reply will fall in the vicinity R, allowing the hitter to move in, make his shot, and continue on to the net.

Consider the receiver. He has been forced back and will be moving forward again.

Yet nine times out of ten the hitter again carefully drives deep. But unless he has a champion's control it is unlikely the ball will pitch deeper than the line L1; it is far likelier to pitch 1 or 2 yds. short of it, so allowing the receiver to continue a smooth forward run, perhaps with the slight swerve to one or the other wing, and hit his passing shot under near perfect conditions.

The ball whizzes by, the crowd applauds and the hitter mentally registers that the receiver has hit a very good shot. Not one in a hundred realises that he could scarcely have made it easier.

What, then, should the hitter do when his very deep drive has forced a short return?

One of the three things. Firstly, if the ball is high enough, hit

75

very hard in an effort to win the point outright or force a weak return for killing.

Secondly, hit a court-opening, angled drive and delay the net advance.

Thirdly, and this is the move of many champions, slice the ball sharply—top liners call it a chip shot—so that the ball pitches at L2 and dies quickly. This they follow in.

Examine now the receiver's situation. He has to rush forward, instead of moving in smoothly, dig the ball up from a low position near the middle of the service line, and attempt to evade the hitter who is hanging over the net.

The lowness of the ball prevents the receiver imparting much speed to it. His forward position seriously restricts the angles available for a pass. And it makes lobbing a matter of great touch.

The secrets of success in this sequence are the depth of the shot to L1, the speed with which the receiver has to rush forward to L2 and the pace and spin of the chip shot; given too much pace it will carry too far after bouncing and so fail to hurry the receiver. Hit too slowly, its pace through the air will allow the receiver sufficient time to run and yet play with controlled touch either a medium-paced, angled passing shot or an accurate lob.

As in the sequences covered by Figure 18 the receiver must be made to move either hurriedly or in an unexpected direction, or both together. Thus his touch and accuracy are both blunted.

The finest example of this sortie was provided by Mervyn Rose when he easily beat the holder and favourite, Dick Savitt, in the 1952 Wimbledon singles.

Savitt, a flat hitter and relatively slow mover—he is a big man—was utterly helpless against it. Indeed, most flat hitters and/or slow movers are.

Here is one situation where spin, be it slice or top spin, helps to find either the slow or medium-paced angled returns which are the best answers to this particular form of net approach.

Figure 20 shows a defensive situation that crops up probably twice in every five right court points in matches between all classes of players from border-line acceptance to Wimbledon champion class.

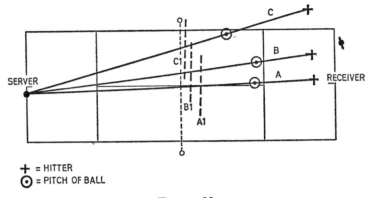

+ = HITTER
⊙ = PITCH OF BALL

FIGURE 20

The server faults with his first delivery and sends over his second ball. It may be almost as good as his first but the receiver will be psychologically attuned to attack and will move in to return the ball deep before advancing on the net.

Most receivers will elect to play their approach shot forehanded, but will not be prevented from advancing behind a backhand, if the second service pitches at A and is struck at the end of the line extending from A. On this return the receiver will reach a net position to give the coverage shown by the line A1.

A tentative second service will pitch in the region of B, will be struck at the end of the line extending from B, and the receiver will reach the net and obtain the coverage shown by the line B1.

Note carefully that there is little to choose between net positions A1 and B1, both of which have been reached by a run roughly parallel with the centre service line.

The defensive key to this situation lies in the server's full realisation that there is little chance of stopping the receiver returning service and moving up to the net.

Of course, occasionally, the second service will be good enough to keep him back but plan in expectation of playing a passing shot or lob next shot.

77

If the receiver is going to move in, what must the server do about it? A little thought will suggest the answer, to make the approach as difficult as possible.

Return to Figure 20 and see what happens when the second ball is made to pitch at C, especially if it carries swerve and slice, something well within the ability of an average player to impart.

The receiver will have to make his return at the extension of the line running back from C and run to the net from a point outside the sideline.

If he runs at the same speed as at A and B, he will reach a point to give coverage shown by line C1.

This leaves a very big gap on the backhand side of his court, either for a passing shot or lob.

If he rushes to protect that side of the court he lays himself wide open to a 'wrong footing' passing shot or lob back towards the spot C or deep in the forehand corner.

The success of this method is dependent on the second service not being so weak that it can be cracked for a winner; after all, it does go to the forehand, usually a man's stronger hitting wing. He will hit a number of winning returns of service but, with the proviso about very weak second services in mind, the number of winners will not compensate for the loss of a commanding net position ensured by this method.

As in previous sequences, the thoughtful reader will already have realised that the system can be used equally well in ordinary rally play.

The finest use of it I ever saw was by Angela Buxton against Darlene Hard in the final of the 1956 London Championships on Grass.

Miss Hard's net rushing had gained her a straight set victory on the hard courts at Sutton. Realising that if she could not keep Miss Hard away from the net on a hard court, she certainly would not be able to do so on grass. Miss Buxton agreed to use these tactics. Forced to make all her net advances from outside one or the other set of tram-lines, Miss Hard was tied in knots by a mixture of passes into the gaps, 'wrong foot' returns to the side from which she had run, and lobs, so losing in two straight sets as easily as she had won their previous encounter.

The surest way of limiting the angles open to the opponent is in returning the ball deep down the middle of the court, point C in Figure 21. In actual play C will move slightly left and right of C, depending on the position on the court from which the man designated 'attacker' in Figure 21 makes his shot.

To put it precisely, in order to reduce the angle open to the defender, return the ball so that it bisects that angle.

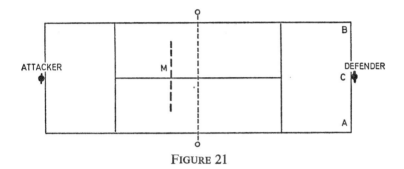

FIGURE 21

Figure 21, however, is shown in order to reveal how a volleyer can reach the net with the greatest degree of safety against a defender with strong passing shots.

In this example I am leaving it to the reader to fill in his own angles and the varying net positions the attacker will take, depending on whether his approach shot pitches at A, B or C.

It will be found that C gives the defender least room for a passing shot against an attacker midway along line M.

The defender can, of course, play his shot without moving though that is not always an advantage; some men are happier hitting on the run than when standing.

Unless the approach shot is deep this 'centre theory' may backfire and just as a shot to C reduces the defender's angles, so his position in the middle of the baseline reduces the angles open to the attacker at the net. Thus the volleyer who uses centre theory extensively will need more volley punch than the man who comes up on drives to the corner; providing he can reach the passing shot he has great chasms of open court into which he can guide his volley.

With the possible exception of the sequences covered by Figure 20, average players are seldom sure enough returning service to net rush continually—these sequences are as applicable to club standard tennis as to higher grades.

Note, however, that they assume net attacks behind shots which are either aimed at the opponent's backhand or down the middle of the court.

Many players up to Wimbledon champions are only really happy volleying behind such shots. They feel off balance and awkward when advancing behind shots to the opponent's forehand corner. This is a weakness which should never be allowed to develop, especially because the most common shot in ordinary levels of tennis is ideally suited to the beginning of three sequences of shots which are prolific point winners.

The common shot is one which is directed at medium pace somewhere towards the backhand corner. Seven times out of ten it pitches approximately at point S in Figure 22.

Nine out of ten players base the direction of their shots on the position of the opponent, keeping part of their eye on him, the rest on the ball.

This is a mistake. The opponent moves and so does the ball.

Yet there are certain very visible and important factors across the net which never move—the lines which form the boundaries of the court.

So as early as possible begin thinking in terms of these lines, using them as the positions on a chess-board to out-guess and out-manœuvre the opponent. Forget the opponent. Learn instead the geometry of the tennis court. Learn it so thoroughly that merely by judging your own position you can hit the ball to within 3 in. or so of any part of any line the other side of the net.

Even when attacked by a volleyer concentrate on the lines, ignore the man at the net and out-think him as though at chess.

The common return shown by S in Figure 22 is an ideal start.

Few players, even among the champions, possess a strong, reliable and accurate backhand drive straight down the sideline.

Make use of this fact by developing an acutely angled, cross-court backhand return which pitches the ball around A and forces the defender to play his return from roughly A1.

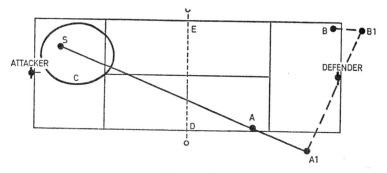

FIGURE 22

Unless he is one of the few with an accurate, down the line backhand shot, the defender's return ball will fall within circle C seven or more times out of ten.

Learn to pitch this at B (whether taken on the forehand *or* the backhand) forcing the defender to run diagonally backwards to make his next shot at B1.

Follow this return to the net, even though it may be the defender's strength. Practise this sequence day after day, week after week until you are equally comfortable volleying all returns, no matter in which direction the ball comes.

This sequence becomes devastatingly effective as soon as a strong backhand drive down the line has been learnt and developed, because the majority of returns from A1 will float back roughly to S.

Sometimes they will be too strong to permit a shot to B; too strong to allow anything but a defensive return.

Sometimes the returns from A1 will permit the start of the sequence shown in Figure 22.

The key shot is the one to A. It must be short, acutely angled and pitched near to the sideline. Then a superior position is established, whether or not the sequence is continued.

To prevent the defender settling down to a fixed routine, vary the second shot (the one to B) with 'wrong-foot' returns back to A and drop shots pitched at D and E.

Some readers may feel these sequences destroy thought and make for a stereotyped state of play. Since with the variations

81

there are about ten sequences to be learnt, I feel no charge of stereotyping can be sustained.

I have also found that once a player starts to think sequentially he soon develops many ideas of his own.

Sequence play has two other immense advantages. The first is in offering a thoroughly practised and almost automatic routine on which to fall back when numb with nervousness or anxiety. It is amazing how a thoroughly drilled system works almost on its own, irrespective of the state of the operator.

The second is that playing 'chess-board tennis' forces the opponent to run and turn far more than haphazard play, so markedly increasing his tiredness and decreasing the resistance he can offer towards the end of the final set, should one be necessary.

These sequences are extremely applicable in every class of women's tennis and, in fact, have been proved successful over and over again.

They are also very applicable in most classes of men's tennis, though in the very highest classes of play the certainty and prevalence of the serve and volley attacks reduce the frequency with which they can be used.

However, on hard courts men like Rod Laver, Manuel Santana and Nicole Pietrangeli use those illustrated and many of their own.

To practise them best, find two other enthusiasts, posting one to play the first return and having the other already in position for the following shot (e.g. in Figure 22 one man could stand at A1, the other at B1).

In working out other sequences remember two things, few players are as happy running up and down the court as they are running from side to side and most are weaker hitting after turning than after running straight.

9

Practice

There are many players who derive as much pleasure from practising as they do from actual participation in competitive matches. This is splendid because one must never forget that the primary social purposes of tennis are recreation and the provision of exercise.

Let me here interject that there is now evidence suggesting that a man who exercises throughout his life increases his chances of longevity and certainly prolongs his active life.

However, in the minds of most people, the object of practice is improvement, and this is the context which must be studied.

What happens when one practises a shot which needs strengthening in order to withstand the pressures likely to be met in competition? Often the weak link lies on the backhand side.

Usually the aspirant to advancement persuades a friend to go out on the court to hit shot after shot at the wing which needs strengthening. It is here that very many little known factors come into operation.

The first point to emphasise is that it is just as easy to practise and become grooved in a faulty technique as it is in one which is sound. Once the grooving has been established, two problems have to be solved—ungrooving or unlearning the faulty technique, followed by learning the correct one.

It is as well, perhaps, to understand how grooving takes place and this I cover in another section of this chapter dealing with mental rehearsal. Sufficient here to record that when the brain 'instructs' a muscle or set of muscles to perform a series of movements, it does so with a stream of electrical impulses.

In passing, the Russians have discovered that the speed at which these impulses travel cannot be increased but the intervals between the impulses can be shortened.

Each repetition of the movements eases very slightly the following passage of nerve impulses—burns a pathway as it were —and the difficulty of eliminating that neural 'pathway' and substituting another logically increases the more it is 'burned' into the system.

This should suffice to show how vitally important it is to practise the technically sound shot and not one which is in conflict with flexibility, adaptability, fluency, good timing and the control of spin, placement, pace, altitude, etc., imparted to the ball.

For this reason I believe it to be important even for near beginners to look beyond the immediate stage of improvement at which they are aiming. This stage should, in the majority of cases, be attainable through the use of techniques which will be all too vulnerable to exploitation by opponents two or three stages farther along the road.

This is one reason why I believe it to be so important for all who are at all keen about tennis to see the world's best players in action. Television makes this simple but television is only a substitute; one learns more and gains added pleasure from actual attendance. Through watching top performers one can comprehend far better the precise skills and techniques required in high level tennis and perhaps acquire the inspiration to ape them oneself.

Many Wimbledon champions swear by the value of watching good tennis and Jaroslav Drobny, Fred Stolle and Manuel Santana are but three 'greats' who watched in the very best possible manner—by ballboying at important championships.

The other sensible precaution against the acquisition of bad techniques (with attendant neural problems over and above 'grooving') lies in taking professional coaching. In Britain today there are over 200 professionals who have satisfied strict examining panels of their teaching abilities. Their names and addresses are obtainable from the Secretary of the Lawn Tennis Association, Barons Court, London, W.14.

Convinced, I hope, of the dangers of unsupervised or unthinking traditional methods of practice, you should be willing to delve yet a little deeper into the psychology of learning.

Learning derives from remembering but there is a vital facet of this which is known in psychology by the rather clumsy title *reminiscence*. To understand this better, imagine an experiment. It is an experiment which has been repeated many times and the results measured under strict laboratory conditions.

The subject is set a physical skills task unlike anything he has ever before met. His performance at the task can be measured or counted precisely. He is put to work, note made of his progress and when he becomes tired—say after seven or eight minutes—he is stopped and made to relax in conditions which do not permit him to think unduly about what he has been doing.

After ten minutes or so he is returned to the task and something rather unexpected is discovered. Instead of resuming with a degree of skill similar or a little below that at which he stopped, the subject will often show a distinct improvement. Indeed, if he had begun the task in a highly motivated state of determination to succeed, his post-rest improvement over pre-rest performance may be quite staggering.

The theory underlying this strange phenomenon necessitates a distinction between performance (i.e. actually performing the task) and habit (i.e. the organisation of the central nervous system so that the task can be performed).

It should be clear that no matter how skilfully the task can be performed, it won't be performed at all unless the subject decides to do so.

In mathematical terms, then

$$\text{Performance} = \text{Habit} \times \text{Drive}$$

However, once the task is begun it seems that a further nervous reaction takes place—rather akin to the increase of resistance to an electric current in a wire as the temperature of that wire rises—which gradually inhibits the action.

This reaction is known as *reactive inhibition* and it is thought by psychologists to be the objective reality which lies behind boredom and also behind fatigue in those tasks where the work load is fully covered by aerobic capacity. (See also page 114.)

This reactive inhibition works against inner drive, first spoiling performance and, when its total equals drive, bringing the performance to an end.

Sometimes this stop will be conscious and voluntary, but often the subject will pause momentarily without even realising it himself.

This has been proved by tests in which the performing subject has been charted on an electro-encephalogram. This 'brain message' measuring machine shows patterns during poor performance and momentary pauses which are identical with those produced during sleep. Here, perhaps, is the reason for so many missed sitters and, maybe, for some motor-car accidents.

Now, the greater the motivation, the greater the reactive inhibition, but the quicker it dispels with rest and the greater is the jump forward in post-rest performance. Thus are shown the importance of motivation and the importance of correctly phasing a practice session.

On the whole, introverts tend to produce reactive inhibition more slowly than extroverts and so are more liable to show 'stick-at-it-iveness'.

How, then, can this be translated into a practical plan for on court training? Each man and woman must discover his or her optimum work-relax cycle, but when seriously intending to develop one particular shot or movement I would suggest eight to ten minutes of highly purposeful application should generate a 'waking-sleep' degree of reactive inhibition and that a complete rest should then be taken from that shot. After ten minutes of rest, reminiscence will result in a step forward—if the technique of the shot is good. Remember, one can equally strongly groove a poor shot.

Rest may be obtained by switching to some other facet of the game, for example, from backhand to serving or volleying, but I consider it should be to something a little gayer than shot development, say ten minutes of 'goals'. After all, one should derive happiness from playing, both from a sociological aspect and from the motivational angle. A normal person wishes to continue and improve when he is enjoying himself. Indeed, I rate happiness from playing as the strongest motivator of all.

The attentive reader may now be wondering how this relates to the long hours of practice indulged in by the Australians who are undoubtedly the most successful tennis nation in history.

For this it must be understood that there are two types of reactive inhibition, perceptual and muscular. Perceptual applies where the brain is being used as a 'translator' of ideas into actions, e.g. when learning a new shot or regrooving an old one.

Muscular reactive inhibition occurs when the perceptual part has virtually ceased, i.e. when a shot has become fully grooved and completely automatic.

It is far slower developing than perceptual reactive inhibition.

To make things crystal clear, when striving to develop a 'grooved' or 'regrooved' stroke, work in relatively short, go-stop phases as this speeds learning considerably.

Once the stroke becomes completely automatic lengthen the 'go' phases. After all, one cannot stop to allow inhibition to dispel in the middle of a match.

One can, however, relax and take ample time between points, though in advocating an 'on and off' system of concentration I am treading on very dangerous grounds. Nevertheless, one of the notable features about so many champions is an instinctive ability to 'pace' their matches correctly.

This truly is an instinct because I doubt if more than a handful of players in the world know the theory which lies behind this. Now, at least, readers should be able to apply intellectually knowledge they lacked instinctively.

Phased practice demands self-discipline and intense will to succeed; it is so much easier to hit a few forehands and backhands and then enjoy a couple of sets while indulging in the self-delusion that this is good match practice.

It is impossible to overstress the major part mental discipline plays in improvement and I make no apology for returning to the point in discussing another valuable way in which it can help the grooving of strokes or methods. It is particularly applicable to people with limited chances of winter practice.

But first the reiteration of a general principle of learning which is so logical that most people know it instinctively.

Put in its broadest sense and with, perhaps, too much simplification, this says that if—to use figures instead of symbols—a total of 24 hours is available for learning a skill—a backhand drive?—the end result from 48 daily sessions each lasting half an hour will be better than from 3 daily sessions each of 8 hours duration.

Undoubtedly there is a point of optimum balance between many short and a few long sessions but, as a general principle, numerous short sessions are better than a few long ones. Remember reactive inhibition?

To return to mental discipline, Billie-Jean King spent one hour of each day during the winter of 1964–5 on her own. She used the solitude to concentrate her mind on the techniques she intended—and eventually did—use in the later months of 1965.

In pre-World War Two days the former British Davis Cup player Donald MacPhail spent one winter 'thinking' his forehand into an improved groove.

Is there any scientific justification to support their claims that the 'thinking sessions' helped their improvement?

Firstly, there is now abundant evidence that the passage of a nerve current through a chain of nerves—caused, perhaps, through the execution of a forehand drive—does not leave that chain of nerves unchanged.

The modification seemingly takes place primarily at the synapses; a synapse is the point of communication between two nerve cells. These are the points where the 'messages' are passed from one set of nerves to another and the modification which takes place simplifies the subsequent passages of similar 'messages'. In tennis language, 'grooving' slowly takes place.

It is possible that this phenomenon is at the roots of all learning, conditioning and habit.

Thus constant repetition of a movement gradually improves the efficiency of the nerves in repeating that movement—be it a good or bad movement.

But this refers to repetition of an actual movement, so how does this link up with imagining?

For this it is necessary to refer to some experiments carried out in America. In these experiments electrodes were attached to human 'guinea-pigs' and connected to very sensitive amplifiers which measured the 'nerve currents and patterns' when the 'guinea-pigs' performed specific movements.

The 'guinea-pigs' then had the particular limbs—sometimes it was their arms—fixed down and they were instructed to imagine themselves repeating their test movements. Remember, they could not move.

The 'nerve currents' produced by imagination tallied precisely with those recorded when the actual, physical movements were made.

It is, therefore, a logical deduction that 'grooving' of the neurons and synapses also took place.

Certainly this provides a scientific reason for the improvements noted in the cases cited by Mrs. King and MacPhail, by others in tennis and particularly by golfers.

Such 'mental grooving' is far from easy to achieve for it requires considerable self-discipline to take oneself off to a quiet spot every day for, perhaps, fifteen minutes. Even greater self-discipline is needed actually to concentrate on mental stroking for that period.

In order to test the truth of this, put down the book, empty your mind of all thought and then try to keep your mind a complete blank for one minute. Stray thoughts will come stealing in after very few seconds and it will take a fair degree of control on your part not to follow one of these 'strays' in the first three-quarters of a minute. If you can keep your mind a blank for two minutes you should be sufficiently disciplined mentally to stand a promising chance of using 'mental grooving' to advantage.

There is, of course, a limit to the amount of improvement that can be achieved in this way. Ultimately the stroke has to be executed in synchronism with a moving ball which had been hit with the intention of evading your reach or disrupting your stroke. So practice on a court with a ball is essential. Nevertheless a great deal can be achieved in the mind alone, especially in terms of learning new strokes or even in mastering new sequences of placements.

No less important, it is valuable as an exercise in objective concentration and mental self-discipline.

A word of warning. The laws of reactive inhibition still apply, so in 'mentally rehearsing' new groovings work in fairly short 'go-rest' phases.

I have now covered fairly thoroughly a theory which should allow any ordinary player to improve quickly and markedly—if he applies that theory correctly.

It should be recalled why one must take every care to practise the correct technique so as to avoid becoming inexorably grooved in a poor one. As with strokes, so with placements. How often one sees two players standing on their respective junctions of backhand sidelines and baselines religiously trading cross-court backhand drives.

Or standing one on either service line volleying back and forth to one another.

To the uninitiated this may appear good practice. Those with deeper understanding of the problems of transferability know that in reality all they are practising is, in the one case, hitting the ball back and forth to one another in the backhand corners and in the other, volleying to one another.

There is no relationship whatsoever to what they will meet or wish to achieve in match play. They are 'grooving' their placements in just about the worst possible manner.

Specificity is today's 'in' word and this is what must be sought in practice. Transfer in skills through practice is very slight so practice conditions must simulate as nearly as possible those which obtain in tournament play.

The difficulties of transferability and the importance of designing specific exercises for achieving clearly defined ends were ideally presented by Professor Graham Adamson when addressing the 1966 National Fitness for Sport Conference at the C.C.P.R. centre, Bisham Abbey. As recorded on tape, he said: 'Are we using the right tests? Are we measuring the right kind of strengths? I tested Leeds United ten years ago and again last week [ending 16th January 1966]. I thought ten years was sufficient gap to see whether the team lived up to Don Revie's suggestion that they would get far better scores than in John Charles's magic years.

'This was not so. If you looked at the scores of both teams

90

and you did not know who they were you would say these are typical of scores of average, non-athletic University students.

'The tests were of the usual strength variety, namely chins and dips, back strength, grip strength, Harvard step test, and they don't show the strengths that might be present in soccer players.'

The nub of this argument should be apparent to anyone who has seen Leeds United in action, either live or on television. The exercises they undertake for soccer make them supremely fit for soccer, yet when they attempt to transfer those skills and fitnesses to tasks which seem very similar, their scores are no better than untrained academics.

Such are the problems of transferability. Thus is revealed the paramount importance of specificity—of designing training and practice which conform closely to conditions in play. Perhaps one additional piece of evidence is needed. If so, it can be supplied by Allen Wade, Director of Training at the Football Association. Moments after Professor Adamson's words, he revealed that the F.A. had very little knowledge about the effects of much of their training. 'We carry on in the hope that it is doing some good,' he concluded.

Now, fully armed with the theory behind improvement the reader may be able to design his own 'specifics' though in most cases help is likely to be required.

Ideally, practice for grooving strokes or building sequences of shots should be carried out in threes, two players taking it in turns to feed the other with the simulated match situations he requires. Generally, 10 minutes alone is sufficient so that the work-rest (since acting as a feed is a form of rest) phasing is 10–20 minutes.

If one of the three is concerned only with helping and is not interested in self-advancement the two who want to improve may be able to turn and turn about on their own, so giving a 10/10 minutes phasing. And any reader who possesses sufficient drive (motivation) to chase up two others, get them on to a court and, most important of all, to persuade them to concentrate on this form of practice—if he can do all this he may be assured that his motivation is sufficient to cope comfortably with reactive inhibition on a 10/10-minute phasing.

How, then, to proceed once the two ambitious players and one helper are on court? This will depend on individual requirements, but an outline of the practice sessions used to help Angela Buxton's amazingly fast advancement in the 1950's, and of those which helped Louise Brough tune up for several of her Wimbledon winning campaigns, should give some indication.

Working in threes, a typical Angela session was:

TIME IN MINUTES

5	Warm-up period.
5*	Serve wide to the forehand, approach shot deep to the backhand and up to the net.
10*	Acutely angled, cross-court backhand followed by deep backhand drive straight down the line and net advance.
10	Acting as one of the two feeds.
5*	Right court, serve down the middle line, run in and volley deep to backhand corner.
10*	Acutely angled, cross-court forehand drive followed by deep drive to backhand corner and net advance.
10*	Acutely angled cross-court backhand, followed by deep cross-court backhand followed by drop shot.
10	Acting as one of the two feeds.
5*	Kick serve to backhand followed by a 'fader' down the opposite line and net advance.
5*	Fast volleying, always trying to put ball away. Feeds not chasing but firing ball after ball from their hands.
5*	Smash followed by volley.
15–25	Set of top speed singles.

In the sequences marked with an asterisk the two feeds control their returns so as to set up the desired situations but they also vary them sufficiently to keep the receiver alert and guessing a little. These are only a tiny sample of the sequences and strokes that were 'grooved' using this system of practice. It must also be pointed out that the times are approximate; no one walked around with a stop-watch so 5 sometimes became 6 or 7 and 10 varied between, say, 8 and 12; one must keep science as a slave and never let it become a master.

Practice with Miss Brough followed a similar pattern, though she preferred to practise with only one person. Again, the sessions were broken up into ten-minute sections covering such factors as controlling return of service, with special emphasis on attacking—murdering is more descriptive—weak offerings, volleying, serving, ground-stroke placing and so on. She, too, normally ended with a few games played at top speed—seven was often the number.

In such sessions there was little or no static stroke play. Backhand practice was always carried out on the run, the feed moving the ball around the court to ensure this. Volleys were put away, not returned to the feed—except when warming up.

Since those days I have discovered an even better and more stimulating system of volley practice—goals.

In this game the goals are formed by rackets or boxes placed about 5 yds. apart on both service lines. Instead of volleying the ball to each other the players try to volley it between the rackets or boxes, counting a goal each time they succeed. It is an all action, all fun game that rapidly develops speed, agility and the ability to place volleys where the other man isn't. There can be few better ways of ending a serious practice session.

10

Pressures and Nerves

As soon as one begins to compete in tournaments, whether they be at a local club or in the wider field of open events, external pressures start to take effect.

At first they may only come from parents, friends, the coach, club mates. Later on they become more oppressive, especially when the national newspaper writers—and I am one of them—focus attention on a young player.

Irrespective of any views about whether this pressure is good or bad, and most people appear to think it is bad, it must not be forgotten that press men have a first duty to perform, and that is to report both what is happening and what the public are discussing.

Probably pressure is applied, but I cannot help feeling that this is often exaggerated in importance by those who criticise and is used as an excuse by players who cannot withstand stress; thus they seek alibis for failure.

This appears to me to be a variation of a well-authenticated psychological situation in which an individual subconsciously jibs at a task which mentally, perhaps, he feels he should face. He is prevented from facing the task by some outside agency. In other words, an escape mechanism comes into action.

When under pressure, a player who is not confident of his ability may subconsciously want an alibi, and the press obligingly provides one.

This is only a suggestion though it is backed up by a certain amount of fact. In my own case, I can with hand on heart swear that never in my playing days did nice or nasty press comment have the slightest effect so far as feeling pressure was concerned. No doubt this was vanity, but at the time I felt the men writing knew far less than I about what was going on and so I regarded their writings with tolerance, yet I hope without ever feeling superior or ungracious. It was pleasant to be written up as a 'wonder-boy' and vaguely annoying to read that I was useless. But as for feeling pressure, never. I knew only too well in my heart why I had won or lost, played well or badly, and there was no future in trying to place the blame outside myself.

Christine Truman has discussed this with me on several occasions and her outlook approximates to mine. Angela Mortimer dealt with the matter another way the year she won Wimbledon. She bought all the papers, put them safely away and then read them all together when the Championships ended. So did Margaret Court.

This does not imply that I was never nervous, that nervousness did not ruin my performance on all too many occasions, and that other players do not suffer in precisely the same way. Unfortunately I did not discover a valuable system for conquering nervousness until much later in life. The system came in time to play an important part in helping one post-war British Wimbledon champion to change in personality from neuroticism to stability in the space of two years. It is not a simple system, but valuable possessions are usually difficult to acquire.

The first rule is to winkle out the primary cause of the nervousness and frequently, perhaps even always in tennis, this is fear of losing.

The word 'primary' is used advisedly because in many young men and women defeat in itself does not worry them sufficiently to cause an anxiety state. In my experience the majority of well-adjusted young men and women are basically realistic in recognising the merits and demerits of those they compete against. If they feel they have played to the limit of their current abilities and yet have not been good enough to win, they are prepared to be generous in accepting the opponent's superiority.

The key words are 'they are prepared to be generous'. All too often they are not allowed to be. Parents, friends, the disappointed coach, Uncle Tom Cobleigh an' all ask what happened, seek alibis, reasons; perhaps they offer excuses or make unjust accusations about the opponent. The same story has to be told over and over again, usually to a subsequent barrage of argument, blame, blarney and advice—some good, most bad and all driving the loser into an unnatural state.

Thus the first positive stage in the system is, before matches, to face squarely the possibility of defeat—perhaps of defeat by someone who should on known factors be beaten—and to appraise honestly just what effect defeat will have.

In the light of that appraisal decisions can be taken mentally on a course of action to meet this disaster—and that course of action includes coping with the well-wishers who will scratch away at the match like a thousand terriers digging after bones.

Perhaps those mental decisions will involve changes of programme, of training methods, of technique. One need not be too detailed about this. Indeed, one should not, because this can lead to an 'acceptance of defeat' state.

Having looked the worst squarely in the face, one can now start planning to achieve the best, though the word 'now' is far from right. If I may be allowed to go back once more to my own case, planning for the best always began twelve months in advance. Not perhaps twelve months ahead of any isolated match but as a general policy. When the first of January dawned each year my long-term planning for the following year came into operation. Plans for the dawning year had been formulated twelve months back.

Naturally, the current year was not neglected but the planning became tactical rather than strategic. Every possible dangerous opponent had been analysed down to the finest details so that scientific tactical systems could be evolved. Practising these systems was part of the short-term planning. The work was immediate, in contrast to the slower, day by day development of techniques, attitudes, etc., which looked to be necessary for advancement in the following year.

Week by week adjustments of training schedules, playing itineraries, partners, hobbies, relaxations, companions, etc., had to be made but these were adjustments of a wide, general plan, not sudden ideas based on a 'maybe it will work' state of hope.

Thus a long-term, general stability slowly evolved.

There remains the question of the most positive forms of action to conquer or obviate nervousness. These hinge on logic and the acquisition of a sound philosophy of competition.

The logic is simple. All games players know that in the course of, say, one hundred contests they play above their previous best perhaps once, on peak form nine times, terribly badly twice, badly eight times and anything from good to fair the other eighty.

These figures make no claims for laboratory accuracy but are near enough to fact to be recognised by cricketers, footballers, athletes, etc., as well as by tennis players.

Assume now an average tennis enthusiast's annual competitive programme to be ten singles events. Of these he emerges champion on, say, two occasions while playing altogether thirty matches. He loses eight times in the other eight tournaments.

Of this hypothetical programme it is safe to say that twenty-four results could have been forecast with 100 per cent accuracy; he was either far better or far worse than the opponent.

The remaining six matches are the ones which must be considered carefully; but first deal with the predestined defeats.

In what state of mind did he go on court? In my experience nineteen out of twenty players endeavour to play miles above their normal peak form when drawn against an opponent who is known to be two or three classes above them.

If, in the hypothetical programme, six of the eight defeats are inflicted by such opponents, is the enthusiast either playing the percentages correctly or, even more important, giving himself the best chance of improving? Unreservedly I assert 'no'.

Since the average competitor will only play significantly above his normal best once or twice a season, the chances of doing so on any special occasion are heavily against him. In trying to find this chimerical, elusive, 'out of this world' form, he is squandering the chance of measuring his normal best against strong opposition and so learning in valuable detail the steps he must next take on the practice court to move up to this higher standard.

The moral I am making is that the serious player should strive always to play 'par tennis' (his normal best standard) in tournaments, seek constantly to develop higher standards on the practice court, and then bring these into operation in tournaments. Only on the rarest occasions would I recommend a wild attempt to play a far higher standard of tennis than normal peak form.

There is another reason for seeking only to play 'par tennis' when drawn against a supposedly better player. Quite often he will not be so mentally keyed up as when meeting someone of his own reputed class. Possibly he will attempt to show off a little and probably he will concede more mistakes than in a match which he begins more seriously. If one has kept calm and managed to stay more or less on level terms in the early stages, he will attempt to apply extra pressure.

Now, more frequently than might be expected, one's own form lifts to meet this new onslaught. This is the moment when the supposedly better player occasionally flusters and cracks and one walks off the court the winner in a 'shock upset'.

The formula up to the improvement in one's own form was, in my own experience, proved right time after time. The crack in the 'star' opponent came only a couple or so times in a season. But reverting to that hypothetical programme, how pleasing to win two or more matches each season of the eight one was presumably predestined to lose.

How good, too, for the confidence and how revealing of the skills and techniques one has to learn in order to make this sudden attainment of a new, peak form one's normal best. Sometimes this jump to a new peak is permanent.

This is not fanciful theory. It is the system I used during the five-year pre-war period when I won more tournaments than any other Englishman against some of the strongest opposition in Europe, the Continent then dominant in tennis. In each of those five years I won at least two matches against men who, on paper, should have cruised home comfortably.

Logically, too, there are sound reasons for making 'par tennis' one's everyday aim. It leads naturally to a philosophy which minimises nervousness and levels out the excesses of elation and depression caused by victory and defeat, neither of which are helpful to improvement or stability.

In any given situation in life, the best one can hope for, surely, is to perform to the best of one's ability.

One seeks through study and practice constantly to improve that best, but at any particular moment of trial it is finite.

Adapting this to tennis, one's aim must be to go on court in a position to achieve that best.

This means being physically fit and in good practice, well equipped and with full knowledge of the conditions and the opponent, and in being mentally prepared to deal with any unforeseen eventuality.

This does not mean hasty preparation a night or two before the match to be played. True planning for any tournament should begin twelve months or more before that tournament. It starts through practice on the court and adherence to a healthy code of living. Study, discussion, experiment and deep thought all give support.

Perhaps, above all, it depends on the full acceptance of the idea of achieving one's best form and then accepting whatever the result turns out to be.

Logically, one can only expect to do one's best. Once this philosophy is fully accepted a tranquil and stable attitude becomes the reward. Supplement this philosophy with determination to improve that best by constant, intelligent practice and training and one is well along the road to a national top-ten ranking.

Thoughtful readers will, I hope, now realise that the quality of their practice is vastly more important than its quantity.

One hour in which each individual shot is played with all one's mind is infinitely more valuable than four hours desultory play, most of it spent in half-hearted sets.

Never go on the practice court without the fullest determination to come off it a slightly better player.

Never go on the practice court without full knowledge of what is to be practised—and why.

When practising, practise—do not play games and sets. When

the moment comes to play games and sets, strive to extreme limits to win every single point.

Even if the practice partner is someone who can be beaten 6–0, 6–0, still win every possible point.

Winning is a habit and it should be cultivated with every mite of concentration and determination in one's character. Even if leading 6–0, 5–0 and 30 love, go all out for the next two points. Develop and nurture this habit of winning at all costs, no matter how many people it annoys.

Win fairly, however. Cheating, and that brand of near cheating covered by the modern word 'gamesmanship', may sometimes prosper temporarily, but only at the cost of lessening the character of the winner.

Champions like Budge, Kramer and Gonzalez were far too complete and big in character to sully themselves by such methods. Thus their bigness of character blossomed till, in their greatest days, it in itself inhibited opponents, irrespective of their superb technical skills.

These are the stages towards the top of the ladder. Followed religiously, they bring rich rewards of their own, irrespective of any accolades they may yield through the attainment of champion status.

Summarizing the conquest of nerves, the first three stages are: (1) face up to the possibility of defeat; (2) have a plan of action ready in case it happens; (3) plan then to bring about the best; and (4) aim to attain par in actual playing form.

By now I hope readers will be convinced of the wisdom of accepting defeat in a balanced manner and of acquiring the determination, industry and intelligence to make that abstract 'par' represent an actual higher standard of play as each week passes. Then one's conqueror of today becomes the hardly yielding subject of tomorrow and the simple prey of next month.

Simultaneously with all this, there must be a long term plan which gives the utmost assistance to the object of achieving par in every match. This means unswerving attention to details and implacable singleness of purpose in following out all the courses of action that aid improvement. Physical training must be rigorously undertaken, weaknesses in technique inexorably eradicated and replaced by strengths. Strategical knowledge and tactical shrewdness must constantly be increased by thought, observation and intelligent reading. Meals, sleep and relaxation must be regulated sensibly. Late nights, over-eating just before matches, the neglect of significant aches or strains—all such things inhibit attainment of the calm state which permits par form when the score stands at five all in the final set and everything depends on you.

Rackets must always be in as perfect a condition as practicalities permit; those with broken strings should not be left until tomorrow for repair but must be dealt with immediately. Glucose tablets and anti-cramp pills, spare pairs of shoe laces, socks and shoes, a comb, safety-pins, talcum powder and adhesive plaster should be kept in a small air-line type bag which can be carried on court for matches. Clean shirts, shorts and so on should be kept in the changing room ready for a change should there be an interval for rain or other causes. One spare set is not enough because another change will be needed after the singles.

When all these many points, long term and immediate, are observed one has given oneself the utmost chance of going on court and attaining that magical par form, even under the severest stresses.

There can be no question of reproach or doubt creeping in at some playing crisis; no 'if only I had . . .' can steal into the mind and erode away composure and form.

One has done one's best and no man can reasonably expect to do more other than to make his best a little better day by day.

When that best is a true 100 per cent best there can be no room for regrets. Then can one 'meet with Triumph and Disaster and treat those two impostors just the same'.

More, one will have acquired a poise and inner calm of mind that will leave no room for nervousness.

This is not an easy plan but it can be developed day by day and in its development it brings ever-growing tranquillity.

It is not the only system for banishing nerves. The Fred Perrys and Chuck McKinleys of this world appear to be born with an outlook which perceives victory as something for them personally to seize, almost as if by right. They seem to dominate instinctively and anxiety appears to be beyond the scales of their personalities.

There are not many of them but there are literally thousands of players who conform to the average assessment of normality in terms of anxiety, nervousness and the like. I know of no better system for conquering such states than the one I have outlined.

It should be realised that 'par tennis' is not a constant factor throughout a match and it is the reason why I consider the phrase 'never change a winning game' to be one of the most dangerous ever written.

Certainly it is true when playing an opponent in a class markedly below one's own. What about those matches when the opponent is in the same class as oneself?

Against such opponents one starts at a certain tempo and level. Perhaps this is sufficient to run up an early lead. Seven times out of ten this will stimulate the opponent to raise his game. After an interval, one will adjust to this new pace or level, and so one's own game will lift itself automatically. This continues throughout, so that most level matches between skilled adversaries end on a higher level than they begin.

This reasoning suggests that a game which establishes a slender, early lead against someone of one's own class will not be good enough to overcome his increasing resistance or ensure ultimate victory. So the winning game must be changed or, at least, intensified.

This crops up daily in tournaments in a situation known as the '5–2 lead'. Daily in the season tournament matches are lost by players who have led 5–2 in the final set.

Examine in detail why. The man who falls 2–5 down is seemingly beaten. With nothing much more to lose, he relaxes. He also makes one final effort to avert defeat. Perhaps he decides on a strong attack. Maybe he makes a successful effort to eliminate unforced mistakes. Possibly he switches to soft-ball tactics—or drop shots and lobs—or extensive use of angled drives.

Whatever it is, if he is basically of similar standard to the man in front, his relaxation plus change of methods spells danger.

Meanwhile, the man in front may grow either a little too confident—or a little too careful.

He may even relax a little stupidly. Suddenly the 2–5 becomes 4–5—often only one service break is involved—and the man in front has lost his advantage. He needs now to break service again to finish the match and so grows overanxious.

All mental ascendancy has changed courts and in the space of about ten minutes 2–5 has become 7–5.

What is the answer? Really it begins sometime before the 5–2 position is reached. Take the case where the first set has been won fairly easily with a strong all-court attack. This, logically, will be countered in the second set so this countering must be frustrated. The safest method in my experience is a slight intensification of the first set attack through moving fractionally nearer to the pitch of the ball.

Taking the ball earlier will hustle the opponent a little more and so increase his difficulty in immediately starting his counter-attack—and once a few games of the second set have been played the psychological timing will no longer be right for the opponent.

On one's own side of the court, the extra concentration needed in taking the ball a shade earlier will not leave room for anxiety or worry about what the opponent is doing. It is a system I have proved over and over again.

However, if the 5–2 situation has not been avoided, what then? Appreciating now the reaction and reasoning of the nearly beaten opponent, it is again clear that an intensification of effort is required. If serving, one must keep pressure on the opponent by getting the first ball in court. If he is basically nervous, force him to create his winning positions and do not give him targets which allow the rallies to end briefly. If he is adventurous, do not risk ceding the attack. Serve or hit for depth and go in to the net. Maintain a steady pressure and do not try to jump up the tempo too dramatically.

In a nutshell, all these situations demand a lively understanding of what is happening and then thought. Seek to use strong shots and do not panic if points have to be fought for far more bitterly than at any time in the match. Do not believe that the winning game played so far will still capture that vital last game.

The most complex example of this reasoning I know was worked out by G. D. Oakley and me when he was fighting for a place in the Davis Cup team and had to meet his chief obstacle in the Hard Court Championships.

The man in question was strong all round but liked to play at an even tempo and was a slow starter.

So the plan was to vary the pace and height of all services and shots for one set, principally keeping the game slow, and then, irrespective of its outcome, to switch immediately to a strong attack.

The plan worked perfectly, for the variations of the first set robbed the opponent of the even tempo on which he thrived and so helped to lengthen the period of his always slow start. Then, when he had finally accustomed himself to the system, the sudden shock of a surprise and strong attack threw him completely out of rhythm again.

So Oakley, who had never before beaten this man, won in three straight sets, only the first of which went into 'games all' (beyond 5 all).

All this is complex, but tennis is a far more complex game than most people realise. Mastery of the philosophy and theories here outlined demands a long and intensive effort of will and mind. But after two years of this effort the habits will have been formed and a very long stride taken towards attaining a high percentage of whatever your personal peak potential may be.

And this, let me emphasise, is normally very considerably higher than one believes.

11

Concentration

Earlier I presented the equation Performance = Habit × Drive. Possibly the most important factor in developing habit is concentration; only through complete application of mind and effort during practice and training is good habit (technique) likely to be acquired.

Similarly, drive will be wasted if concentration is poor though it may be justifiably argued that strong drive rules out all chance of poor concentration.

This is not strictly accurate. It is possible to be both strongly motivated and excessively nervous, in which case concentration is likely to wander. This alone is one reason for learning and acquiring techniques which aid concentration. This calls for self-discipline.

Probably the first exercise in developing good concentration lies in keeping one's eyes within the confines of the court. This does not in itself prevent stray, distracting thoughts from invading the mind when it should be fully concerned with overthrowing an opponent, but it does inhibit an important sensory medium of thought stimulation—the surrounding scene. The eyes are a profuse source of mind activating sensations. If they are trained to look at neutral things, e.g. the ground, they cannot see the pretty blonde in the front row of seats and set one contemplating the chances of getting a date.

Angela Mortimer, whose concentration remains a byword, rigidly trained herself not to look outside the court and she asserts that this was the first step in learning to concentrate.

Fred Stolle was told by his father he had bad concentration and would never achieve success until it improved.

Unfortunately one can be distracted by factors other than the crowd. Incorrect umpire's calls are a good example.

It is simple to advise 'ignore them' but this is not always easy. In any case, ignoring something is a negative process. Better by far to have a positive attitude, and again I believe Miss Mortimer found the ideal solution. When robbed of a point by a faulty decision she immediately thought to herself: 'That's one point you shouldn't have got. I'm not going to let it become two by worrying about it and losing the next point as well.'

So she immediately redoubled her efforts to win the next two points. This suggests there are various types of concentration, a fact I dealt with in an article published in *Sport and Recreation*.

Before reproducing this with acknowledgments to the magazine and its editor, I will enumerate one or two things an average player can do to combat waning concentration. All entail positive action, which is in itself an antidote to nervousness as well as a marshaller of attention.

They are:
(1) Try to see the seam of the ball from the moment the server picks it up until you hit it.
(2) Bounce the ball a few times.
(3) Take half a dozen deep breaths to a count of six, exhaling in one second each time.
(4) Decide to take the ball just after the top of the bounce.
(5) Walk slowly between points for a few games.

And now for the article which was entitled 'Concentration, the Stuff of Champions' (October 1963 issue) and which, I believe, tells all that one needs to know of the theory of concentration.

'Harry Hopman, the man more responsible than any other for Australia's long domination of the international tennis scene, has frequently said that success on the courts evolves 25 per cent from strokes and 75 per cent from mental factors.

'To those involved deeply in the highest levels of championship play this is now a well recognised truism though it has not always been thus; only at the start of this year did the Lawn Tennis Association change its official policy for choosing youngsters for special training, the propensity for winning—no matter at what age—superseding the old system in which a child's ability to hit fluent shots was rated ahead of its concentration and determination to hang on and win by the best means at its command.

'The importance, too, of these mental, temperamental and physical factors is scarcely comprehended at quite advanced tournament levels, except by the few who progress to positions near to or in the world's first ten.

'This, perhaps, is an oversimplification; in a survey carried out by *British Lawn Tennis* magazine some years ago, 90 per cent of the players interviewed gave concentration as one of the most important factors in tennis. It is when one probes deeper in seeking understanding of concentration that one finds vital differences between the champions and those who play a similar amount of tennis without ever achieving the same heights or proficiencies.

'During thirty-five years, playing, coaching and writing about tennis, I have concluded that concentration can be divided into four categories, that is if one takes the relative lack of concentration to be found in many dabblers and "play for fun and social contact" exponents as one of those categories.

"Progressing upwards, the degrees of concentration can be described as: (2) subjective, (3) objective and (4) applied.

'While the dabbler can never—or scarcely ever—achieve the heights of applied concentration found in a Ken Rosewall, Jaroslav Drobny, Chuck McKinley or Angela Mortimer, it is all too apparent that top liners can often be brought down to the dabblers' class by extraneous events; of these, poor or dubious decisions and calls by umpires or linesmen head the list.

'One or two examples will help to define the categories a little more specifically. Most readers will have seen typical dabblers at play, if not at tennis then in other games. Ever ready for a chat or a look at the blonde passing by, the effort they apply to the game itself is negligible, as is their rate of progress.

'But sometimes from this group arise those who wish to improve and some become aware of a need for better concentration. I would be a much richer man if someone could give me £1 for every youngster I have heard muttering on court, "I must concentrate, I must concentrate" or, more simply, "concentrate".

'This is the most elementary type of subjective effort and it only needs a moment's thought to realise that the effort of concentrating is in itself a distraction from the game in progress.

'Fred Stolle, winner of the Wimbledon doubles in 1962 and runner-up in the singles this year, found a more advanced form of this type of thing useful this year. He told me, "My father has always said my concentration is bad and I certainly seem to see everything that is going on around. So this year I made up my mind that as soon as each point ended I would look at my feet. That way at least I'd keep my eyes within the court."

'In fact, Stolle also used applied concentration extensively, but at the level keeping his eyes on his feet did little to improve the basic performance of which he was capable.

'Yet great oaks from little acorns grow, and for any ambitious young player suffering a wandering mind this is a good piece of practical advice.

'The principle was recognised by Angela Mortimer who, in 1961, was the last English player to win a singles championship at Wimbledon. Long famed for her concentration, Miss Mortimer does not believe she is especially endowed in this direction. She told me recently, "Just as a boy or girl at school starts arithmetic with simple tables, so the first exercise in concentration is learning to keep one's eyes within the court. The moment they catch sight of things outside the court they set up thoughts in the mind and these detract from those which one is giving to the match. After this has become second nature, one becomes free to think about tactics and so on, but learning to keep one's eyes within the court takes quite a long time."

'Whether it is looking at one's feet or not letting the eyes roam outside the court, the exercise is one of self-descipline more than anything else.

'There is still ample room for nervousness, uncertainty and worry to come creeping in, as was discovered by Margaret

Smith,[1] the greatest woman player ever to come from Australia and unquestionably the world's number one today.

'Miss Smith came to Wimbledon as outstanding favourite in 1961, 1962 and 1963, only to crash badly the first two years before winning at the third attempt.

'I have watched Miss Smith play dozens, if not hundreds, of matches without ever seeing her eyes stray from the court. Yet this did not stop her suffering from excessive nervousness with a consequent diminution of form.

'An intelligent young woman, Miss Smith faced this problem squarely and early this year found a solution. "When I lost to Christine Truman in 1961 and Billie-Jean Moffit[2] in 1962, I worried because I was playing badly even though I was winning," she analysed: "so I decided this year that instead of worrying whenever I found my concentration wandering I would tell myself to watch the ball more closely or to move my feet around. I've a one-track mind and cannot think of more than one thing at a time. But by concentrating on one thing I have learnt how to overcome my nervousness. It helped me enormously at Wimbledon."

'There are many variations of the Stolle system, with bouncing the ball before serving as one of the most popular. Likewise, many players try watching the ball more closely but this requires more skill than is generally realised, and therefore is not always so effective as with Miss Smith.

'Before moving on to the "applied" category, the question of time needs consideration.

'This can be divided into two categories, the first covering advance concentration on a particular tournament, the second on a given match.

'Last year, the red-headed Australian Rod Laver equalled a 24-year-old performance set up by another red-head, Donald Budge, when he completed the tennis "grand slam" in winning the four major championships in the world, namely the Australian, French, Wimbledon and American. Of these, all but the French are contested on grass courts which, contrary to popular

[1] Margaret Court
[2] Billie-Jean King

opinion outside tennis circles, are far faster than the red hard courts which are standard in most parts of the world.

'Laver was reasonably confident that he could win on grass but feared the fortnight in Paris. So immediately after winning the Australian title in mid-January he began quietly experimenting with shots and tactics which would help him surmount this particular obstacle.

'This was a situation in which it would have been simple to have lazed in a false belief that he was experimenting. In fact he lost surprisingly on one or two occasions, but this was through ill health. His experiments were made with a very quizzical mind and by the end of May, when the French Championships finished, Laver had developed a fine technique for hard court tennis.

'I believe that the new strokes and systems a player is learning or practising at any given moment only become really effective twelve months or so later and that generally at the earliest.

'Players vary enormously in the pre-match time they take to achieve full concentration. Maureen Connolly, possibly the greatest woman player in history, would mentally leave her companions a good two hours before any particular match, all but the loudest of questions sailing right over her head. During that time she would be applying more and more of her mind to the coming match and the methods she would use to win it. Just as it took her a long time to wind up, so she needed a winding down period and it was customary for her to go straight to another court after winning, merely to hit a ball about until the unwinding was complete, generally in half an hour. She even did this after winning Wimbledom, to the amazement of all but the handful of friends who knew her well.

'Miss Mortimer is another who liked to build up slowly to a match but there are a few who become very nervous if they dwell too long on matches to come. More than anything else, it seems, the right moment to begin concentrating depends on the individual.

'Billie-Jean Moffit, runner-up to Miss Smith at Wimbledon this year, spent fifteen minutes of each day last winter detachedly contemplating tennis concentration and avers this was responsible for the great improvement over 1962 that she showed in this field. Her contemplations took her into the field of applied concentration and here the opportunities for advancement are limitless.

'Two factors must be mastered before applied concentration can be fully effective. Fistly the eye and mind should remain automatically within the bounds of the court. Secondly technique—Hopman's 25 per cent of tennis success—must be completely automatic and fundamentally sound. Then the mind can be given over to the task of making the utmost use of the assets at one's disposal.

'How this works is best demonstrated by some factual examples, the first of which took place in the 1954 Wimbledon singles final.

'After almost three hours of intense play Jaroslav Drobny had reached match-point against Ken Rosewall. Throughout the final Drobny had been serving at great speed. As he walked back for this, the most crucial point on the whole of his long career, he reasoned: "On such an important point Rosewall will be set for something extra fast and for me to run to the net behind it. If I serve slowly he will have time to spot the difference and adjust himself." So Drobny served a spinning ball at three-quarters speed while remaining at the back of the court. Momentarily surprised, but without time to realise fully what was happening, Rosewall mistimed his shot and his return went into the net.

'This is a simple, one point illustration. When Sven Davidson beat Guiseppe Merlo of Italy in the final of the French Championships a few years ago, I devised for him a plan which required far more subtlety and sustained effort. Merlo, a wizard of control, uses both hands when returning the ball from the normal backhand side. This shortens his reach by the equivalent of one step and so opens up slightly the other side of his court. Consequently, when attempting to pass a man at the net on critical points, he normally aims straight down the line. On points that are not critical he chances pulling the ball across the court, even though he may not be quite on balance.

'Davidson, like the majority of tennis players, builds his net

111

game on shots directed to his opponent's backhand and feels somewhat awkward when approaching behind shots to the forehand. However, as he had never won more than three games in a set from Merlo in earlier meetings, something special was called for.

'So he decided to attempt to make use of this knowledge. His task was fourfold: first, to restrain his natural tendency to attack the backhand from the net; second, to realise clearly during play which were the critical points; third, to play his first shot to the backhand before going up to the net on the following shot deep to the forehand; and fourth, to control his balance well enough to volley effectively balls coming at angles which he naturally found awkward.

'Such is the quality of Davidson's concentration that he selected 13 points for this particular routine, winning 11 of them and beating Merlo for the first time in his life. Incidentally, this was the first time that a Swede won one of the world's major titles.

'It can, of course, be argued that these examples show tactical skill rather than special concentration, but this is only half true.

It is relatively simple to devise tactical plans but quite another thing to remember and apply them amidst all the distractions of intense competition.

'Indeed, of all the problems facing British coaches today, this is surely the most difficult. One cannot seriously grumble at the quantity of effort put into tennis by our top and potential top players.

'But how one longs for a quality of effort comparable with that made by most of those who have climbed those extra steps up the ladder to reach the summits of tennis achievement.'

12

Fitness

No matter how perfect a man's technique, tactics and concentration may be, he will not win important championships unless he is physically fit and psychologically and mentally mature and composed. Then, if the motivation is strong enough there is a chance he can grow into a 'good competitor' and a winner of championships.

Though I share the view already given of Harry Hopman, that near-legendary leader of Australian success, that winning tennis is 75 per cent mental and only 25 per cent strokes, I think it is more logical and sequentially correct to deal with physical fitness and training before passing on to the psychological aspects of the game, and finally, the isolation and analysis of the champion's full personality.

First, though, let me try to define what I believe fitness for tennis to be. The simple definition, as given at the 1966 'Fitness for Sport' Conference organised by the Central Council of Physical Recreation, runs 'the ability to undertake the given task without becoming fatigued'.

So far as tennis is concerned, fitness entails a great number of factors:

(*a*) Endurance;
(*b*) Speed;
(*c*) Balance;
(*d*) Strength;
(*e*) Flexibility;
(*f*) Agility;
(*g*) Visual aucity;
(*h*) Technical skill.

However, for the moment I will stay with the definition 'ability to do work'.

The work that any man can do is proportional to his oxygen uptake per unit of time, so the major criterion of fitness is the rate of oxygen uptake.

This is not strictly proportional to lung capacity. The lungs have to feed the oxygen into the blood in order that the blood may dispel the lactate which accumulates in working muscles.

If one could so train that the oxygen content of the blood stayed ahead of the demand set up by lactate, the athlete could go on playing indefinitely. This, in fact, must be the aim of the player who is training, to increase his 'cruising speed' till it can be met exclusively by aerobic capacity.

In fact, this would not enable a man to go on performing indefinitely; reactive inhibition of the muscles must be considered, though in a highly fit and skilled technician, backed by extreme motivational drive, this stage of apparent fatigue can often be pushed well beyond completion of a set competitive task.

There is another aspect of training which is often overlooked when considering the question of fitness. It is the acquisition of sheer skill in stroke making.

One runs miles per day in order to increase endurance. The demands on that endurance, however, are lessened when the technique is efficient, smooth and rhythmic. To be specific, even to an unpractised eye it must be evident that a player with the smoothness of, say, Fred Stolle, must make lower demands on internal physical energy than a cruder stroke maker, e.g. Cliff Richey, all other things being equal.

In fact they seldom are. Often the cruder player will be more highly motivated than the fluent stylist. Quite possibly he will also be more introverted. With those two qualities he will resist far more strongly the onset of reactive inhibition and so overcome overt fatigue with more apparent readiness.

Physical fatigue set up by lactate in the muscles can be neutralised to some extent by taking glucose. In very rough terms, one glucose tablet neutralises the fatigue set up by one average game of tournament tennis.

It must be fully realised that glucose cannot improve one's basic fitness. If basic fitness is represented by 100, sensible glucose intake will enable a player to stay near to 100 for a longer time than if he had not taken glucose.

Actually, many doubts about training and its effects have been expressed recently in research units.

With Professor Graham Adamson, the father of circuit training, at their head, the doubters are saying, in essence, that they do not know if training increases fitness or merely eliminates the inhibitions which prevent us releasing all the forces dormant within us. They cite the immense strength demonstrated by men during fits or under the influence of hypnotism.

It may be, of course, that the inhibitions serve a valuable function; without them we might so expend our forces that we damage ourselves.

I have postulated earlier that the 'carry over' in normal training is not very great. For that reason great care should be taken to ensure that training is related as specifically as possible to the individual needs of the trainee.

To return to my specifications for tennis fitness, how can each of them be aided?

I go all the way with Geoffrey Dyson. What a tragedy it was for this country that he was allowed to go to Canada; but it seems the fate of all progressive thinkers to be viewed with suspicion by national sports associations whose members are normally ten to fifteen years behind them in knowledge. Dyson postulates that the mixing of fast and slow running—technically known as interval training—is best of all for the heart and lungs and so for building endurance. Endurance is not so much an inherited as an acquired characteristic. It calls for many qualities; the basic physical condition to pump oxygen into the blood and so keep the muscles free of lactate; the motivational drive to withstand reactive inhibition; the mental power to see tiredness as a challenge to be squashed.

Straightforward running is boring; that must be faced squarely. Yet there is no substitute for it. Through running oneself continually into a feeling of fatigue one develops a callousness towards it. One discovers there is a very real difference be-

115

tween feeling tired and actually being tired. One slowly brings one's psychological peak ever nearer to one's physiological peak. How far should one run? Emerson thinks five miles a day light exercise.

Circuit training, too, is valuable in developing strength and endurance simultaneously. Circuit training consists of performing a succession of carefully designed and related exercises in a given time; usually the circuit is repeated two or three times.

Then over a period of weeks one strives constantly to perform the circuits in ever-lessening time.

One great advantage of circuit training is the spur of competition. One can measure accurately week by week improvement simply by noticing the reduction in time.

A suitable proved 'circuit' is given in Appendix B at the back of this book.

In strength and endurance training one gets out only what is put in. So one must strive to the limits of one's capabilities to work with ever greater intensity or for longer periods. In a nutshell, endurance and strength are gained by maximum quantity as well as quality of effort.

Though many authorities from Professor Graham Adamson downwards are now entertaining doubts about what isotonic (weight) and isometric (straining against an immovable object) training actually achieve, there is a general faith that they help.

In building strength one must guard against putting on weight—one aims to improve the power-weight ratio—and hypertrophy. Hypertrophy of the upper arm, for instance, could ruin a smooth service swing even though the server may have added enormously to his strength.

Heredity determines the number of muscle fibres we possess. Only divine intervention can increase that number, so one seeks to increase their useful size; note 'useful'. In fact, tennis demands power—the ability to supply strength quickly—rather than brute strength.

Speed is very largely an inherited characteristic. One can increase the power-weight ratio and so improve acceleration. One can refine technique until it functions with the smooth efficiency of a jet engine. However, indisputably it is far more difficult to increase muscular speed than it is to improve endurance and strength. Therefore, if lack of speed is proving a handicap, that handicap will be lessened only by really intensive effort.

So far as tennis is concerned, I know of nothing to equal potato races, shuttle running and two against one practice in bringing a player to his upper speed limits.

Two against one practice is described fully in Chapter 9.

Shuttle running takes place between two points A and B 10 yds. or so apart, the pupil trying always to lower his time for 100 yds. run to and fro between the two points.

I believe potato races are slightly more efficacious than shuttle running. Put a bucket down and scatter a dozen potatoes, tennis balls or the like in a circle at distances varying between 6 and 12 yds. from the bucket. Start from the bucket and time how long it takes to put all the potatoes in the bucket. Do not turn always in the same direction. Drive yourself to the limits of your capacity in seeking speed.

This exercise involves starting, running, stopping, twisting, stooping. Worked at with determination and linked with plenty of two against one 'on court' practice it can achieve amazing advances in speed.

So do not be too dismayed if you have only now discovered the problem of speed. Instead, be quite positive and definite in planning to reach your own maximum. The chances are heavily in favour of its proving adequate at the highest level, providing you remain unsatisfied until it is so.

Strength is a function of other factors besides fibre size and quantity. Muscular contractability and motor command are but two of them. However, these are well beyond the scope of this book.

The power-weight ratio plus the contractability factor of the muscles also govern the heights and width which can be jumped, a vital factor in net play.

Again, the 'circuit' of Appendix B contains exercises which should increase elevation. This L.T.A. official circuit has been very carefully prepared and the B.A.S.M. have cleared all the individual exercises from any danger of injuring healthy people.

Many unskilled enthusiasts work away at deep squat jumps with heavy weights across their shoulders in the belief these make the knees stronger.

The knee is a joint, not a muscle, and is particularly susceptible to damage. This was dealt with authoritatively and expertly in a letter I received from Professor Karl K. Klein, perhaps the world's greatest authority on the knee, in March 1965. A campaigner of long standing against dangerous knee exercises, he wrote that while squat exercises in which the thighs were parallel to the floor, or almost so, were acceptable, any squatting action that involved flexing the knees to within the last possible 20–30 degrees, i.e., squatting with the buttocks down on the heels, was harmful. Further, making use of excessively heavy weights in squatting exercises should be discouraged, as this caused the toes to turn out, so that the knees were drawn together between the toes, and consequently both the flexing and the straightening action placed abnormal stresses on the collateral ligament structures and could result in a loosening of the ligaments of the joint. Professor Klein called attention to the excellent illustration of this action in *Anatomy and Ballet* by Celia Sparger (A. & C. Black). It had also been found, he pointed out, that this action had a positive tendency to weaken the long arch of the foot and lead to the development of pronation of the ankle which is detrimental to the efficient functioning of the foot.

With regard to the 'squat jump' exercise, Professor Klein's conclusion was that again it was the depth of the squat that was important. The old type of squat jump—down on the heels—was bad, but if the leg that was behind the other at each jump was only bent to half, or at most three-quarters, of its potential, and the heel was raised, this was an acceptable exercise.

As for the 'duck waddle', Professor Klein remarked that it had been used as a punishment in so many situations that it could not possibly be a good exercise under any conditions!

Professor Klein had just completed a comprehensive study of the growth and development of the ligament structures of the knee, which he was preparing for publication. In the course of this work he made tests on people engaged in all kinds of sport—football, hockey, wrestling, etc.—and those who did no deep-squat training had knee ligaments tighter than the average of their age group, and were almost 100 per cent injury free. Those who did 'squat lifts' had at least 50 per cent more ligament looseness than the average of the comparable group.

Lest there should be any misunderstanding, Professor Klein added a reminder of the difference between the ligaments of the body and the muscles and tendons. While flexibility of the muscles and tendons was an asset to the athlete in terms of injury prevention, ligaments should maintain stability without excessive flexibility.

Professor Klein's work at the University of Texas on the knee has been fully endorsed by the A.M.A. and medical associations the world over.

Flexibility is essential in tennis, not only in its obvious aspects like scrambling, making strokes under pressure or at speed, but also in some ways which are less obvious.

This impressed itself on me very forcibly during a course Al Murray, the British Olympic weight training coach, ran for me some years ago. The pupils ranged from enthusiastic veterans to a few of the most promising juniors of the day.

Murray was demonstrating ankle flexibility and it became immediately apparent that he could straighten his foot with his leg to a far greater extent than any of the pupils. Indeed, in terms of angles, he was able to achieve something like an extra 20 degrees of straightness. Transferring this to terms of horizontal reach, he gained 6 in. or more over the promising juniors.

At low levels of tennis this may not matter overmuch. Imagine, though, moving the lines out a farther 6 in. on either side of the court and then trying to attack Ken Rosewall, Rod Laver, Manuel Santana or Margaret Court from the net. With that extra room for their passing shots they would be gaining as much as one point a game benefit. What a handicap to give players of that calibre!

So ankle flexibility is a must and that goes for knee and hip flexibility, too. The knees and hips are involved not only in reaching, running, stretching, etc., but also in stroke making to a marked degree. Lacking flexibility a player is vulnerable to many returns, e.g. short, sliced 'faders', in-swingers to the body.

Ability to watch the ball and to transfer body weight into the shot is also impaired.

Shoulder, elbow and wrist flexibility affects reach and strokes, especially service. Only with wrist snap for example, can one ever develop a reliable cannon-ball service, and Bob Falkenburg showed in 1948 that a cannon-ball service almost on its own is sufficient to win the Wimbledon singles.

So rotational exercises must be included—but they must be related as closely as possible to the specific tennis tasks envisaged. I cannot overstress how difficult it is to get effective transferability. In athletics, for instance, it has been found that significant increases in leg strength may only be reflected in superior running or jumping performances at the end of a year.

Thus Indian club swinging will certainly improve one's skill in swinging Indian clubs but whether this flexibility transfers to service action is questionable. Better, therefore, to use a racket and repeat the actual service swing itself, seeking always to prolong the length of the back swing and to increase the extent of the racket drop behind the back prior to the actual throwing section of the full swing.

However, there are better exercises for flexibility. For example, twisting exercises with weights so that, to some degree, the momentum of the weights extends the body.

Passive exercising, in which one takes the limb to what appears to be the limit of its stretch and then one stretches a little farther, produces better results than twisting, moving exercises.

Say that I wish to loosen my shoulders and I swing my arm back vigorously. My aim would be to stretch the muscles by the momentum generated in my arm. But physiologists say that under such circumstances other muscles there resist the movement.

However, take the arm to a fully extended, horizontal position and then actively contract the muscles behind—through the reciprocal enervation of muscle, these relax and the ultimate stretching is greater than when using momentum.

This is conscious control achieved by the stretching of muscle and relaxation of its antagonists rather than by hopefully relying on body momentum.

It is not possible to become fit overnight and even if it were the advantages to a really ambitious and determined player would be slender. That is because, in general and rather approximately, one grows unfit in the same time one originally became fit. Thus the man who trained on Monday and was fit on Tuesday would be back to unfitness again on Wednesday. On the other hand the man who begins daily training on October 1st and slowly progresses to a peak by March 31st of the next year will, in normal circumstances, need only marginal 'topping up' to remain on tip-top shape for the season April 1st to September 30th.

I have already written of the way in which glucose helps to offset tiredness.

The effects of massage can be even more dramatic. Research carried out by E. A. Muller on men set a carefully measured work task showed:

Half a minute's massage on each leg gave 27 per cent recovery.

One and a half minutes gave 53 per cent recovery.

Three minutes gave 70 per cent recovery.

The effects would have been still higher if both legs had been massaged simultaneously.

He concludes 'three minutes of massage are enough to bring almost complete recovery to the muscle'.

Seemingly, massage eliminates what he calls 'stopping substances' from the muscles. These lower contraction strengths.

He points out that repeated massage exhausts a muscle's fuel reservoirs and it takes a long time to recover from this.

The practical benefit of this lies in making possible an increased intensity of effort; work possible in eight hours can be concentrated into two to three hours by massage but exhaustion after this is far greater than after eight hours without massage.

Oxygen debt—the state reached when lactate accumulation outstrips oxygen uptake and transfer—oxygen debt recovery time is accelerated if there is light exercise between intervals of work.

All this, I believe, should give the ambitious tennis player an insight into the science of training and some of its techniques. All the reading in the world won't improve his fitness. That can only be achieved through action. Continuous, day by day, week by week, month by month action through heat, cold, rain, snow.

Boredom is the arch-enemy so train with friends.

Devise games to keep the periods happy and enjoyable. Invite parents and other friends along to watch—the Russians do this all the time.

Keep aiming at targets just ahead of current capabilities, moving quickly to the next target as soon as the current one is achieved. Gear training to the attainment of success—but always bear in mind that, in the context of tennis, fitness is not an end in itself but only an instrument for aiding tennis.

Finally, bear in mind that training is an individual matter and no set pattern can apply to everyone.

Each of us is an individual with differing 'specifics'—ideas, attitudes, physiological and psychological make-ups, skills, abilities and so on.

Assess those factors, devise suitable training and then drive like the devil to effect improvement. To be effective fitness training must be worked at with an unremitting determination to derive 100 per cent effectiveness out of every minute of training.

13

The Psychology of Tennis

One can master all the techniques of stroke play, display a professorial understanding of tactics, train to the fitness peak of an Olympic gold medallist, compete in all the right tournaments and yet still fall short of top levels.

There is still, therefore, a quality to be developed. In some, perhaps most top-level players, it appears to be inborn—a genetic hand-down from the right kind of ancestry. Probably the highest degree of this quality is attainable only by those who have been born with it. Yet for any individual to admit this is to concede failure. I have seen many tennis players succeed by eventually acquiring sufficient of this quality to support their technical assets in careers which have reached the highest levels.

They have taught themselves to become 'good competitors', and in this chapter I will attempt to analyse some of the factors which make a 'good competitor'.

Firstly, however, let us define a 'good competitor' in precise terms.

He is a man who, on every critical occasion in which he is participating, tends to bring out the very best performance of which he is capable.

This cannot normally be the case when he is winning easily. Strong pressures will more often arise when the occasion is important and the going is tough—probably when he is playing for his country or his team rather than for himself, so that others will stand or fall by his performance.

This, indeed, is the greatest strain of Davis Cup tennis, so that even the great Fred Perry told me 'the strain of a Wimbledon final is nowhere near so great as that of a Davis Cup Challenge Round'.

This view is shared by 99 per cent of all who have played Davis, Federation or Wightman Cup tennis. Rare indeed are the men and women who thrive when they are playing for anyone or anything other than themselves.

Whether one is by heredity a good competitor or if that state has been reached through a long process of philosophical detachment, it should be fully realised that this is not a constant state.

It was first spotlighted by Lord Moran during World War One when he realised that many men convicted of cowardice were, in fact, utterly incapable of combat at the time. Yet, given a period of rest, they would have recovered completely.

Here let it be recorded that, however great the strain of ten Challenge Rounds rolled into one, it would still be minimal compared to war-time action.

This was understood more fully in World War Two and Figure 23 shows the reactions of R.A.F. air crew as the number of operations increased.

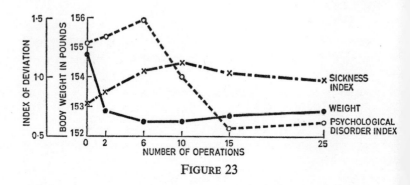

FIGURE 23

The graph measures three factors, (1) sickness set up by mental stress, (2) index of psychiatric disorders, and (3) the effect of stress on body weight. The variations are considerable, in one factor nearing 300 per cent.

The practical tennis lesson to be learnt from this graph is

124

that no player can expect to remain at anything like peak efficiency if he competes in tournaments week after week for months at a time.

The graph became available eighteen years after Jack Kramer won Wimbledon but he, and predecessors like Donald Budge, needed no scientific figures to prove this theory to them.

Kramer has written many times that present-day players compete in far too many tournaments. He told me recently: 'I only used to take part in about twelve a year. I would aim to be in peak condition for three or four major events a year and use the other tournaments as build-ups. If you want to progress you must take time out to practise, eliminate weaknesses and to assimilate what you have learnt from your matches. If you play too much, defeat and victory cease to be important to you.'

Earlier on I cited William James's apt observation: 'One learns to ski in the summer and to swim in the winter.' This can be qualified and adapted to becoming a good competitor during rest or non-competitive periods.

Then, when away from the immediacies of participation, one can mentally savour the atmosphere of top competition. Past experiences can be recalled, analysed, refined and projected forwards into future occasions when victory will be of prime importance.

The atmosphere of those moments to come can be conjured up in the mind and an attitude towards them developed.

Angela Buxton Silk presented a classic example of this the year she won the doubles and reached the final of the singles at Wimbledon. Around 6.30 a.m. on the second morning my telephone rang. Over it a breathless voice said, 'I'm so nervous about playing on the centre court I haven't slept all night. Whatever can I do?'

Because she is a tough-minded, sensible woman, gentle platitudes were out. A positive attitude was needed and her general background provided the key. My answer ran along these lines: 'You are going to play many matches on the centre court, so you must master it at once or it will master you. You understand the stage so think of the centre court as being your natural venue. Imagine you are Dame Flora Robson walking on the stage at the Old Vic. She would take command of the whole situation and would revel in it. So must you.'

The effect was such that she later wrote: 'The only trouble was that afterwards I wanted to play all my matches on the centre court.'

Let me quickly add that one cannot use the same approach with everyone, as I discovered twelve months later when another woman in the world's top ten approached me with almost identical words.

Remembering the past success, I repeated the spiel . . . and the poor woman went on the centre court almost paralysed with fear.

In the first instance, of course, I had been coaching the subject for some years and knew her very well. In the second case my contact was loose and so the advice was snap rather than the result of full understanding.

So in mental rehearsal try to uncover all the snags, fears, hopes and situations which may be experienced. Play the imaginary match on the court on which it will actually be staged. Try to capture the inner feelings that are likely to invade you.

Imagine yourself playing smoothly and well and that the opponent is also in good form and that you are having a tremendous tussle. Fill your mind with the enjoyment of this battle to the exclusion of thoughts of victory or, if not of victory, certainly of defeat.

Beginning twenty-four hours or so before an important event, the picture is usually one of the following two alternatives. In one there is a high state of tension, the mind thinks only of the match and there are likely to be physical manifestations in the form of insomnia, clumsiness, indigestion, bouts of breathlessness, profuse sweating, pressure over the heart and so on.

If protracted, this leads to mental and physical exhaustion before the competition and so ruins performance. In minor forms it leads to acceptance of coming defeat and the generation of excuses which can be offered.

The other picture is one of distraction, the opposite of tension. All thought of the match is avoided, responses to stimuli are unnatural, there will be a tendency to over-eat, play cards, watch television, read, sleep and so on.

This subconscious over-protection prevents limits being approached in the match and so must be guarded against almost as carefully as the overtense state.

In situations like this a trusted, sensible coach or friend can prove invaluable. With him one can, or at least should, be completely honest and in talking out the situation help to alleviate the condition.

In Chapter 9, Practice, I wrote at some length about mental rehearsal. This can be used as effectively in a psychological context as it can in improving technique. By constantly thinking about oneself as a particular type of person, one tends to become that type of person.

This was discovered forty years or so back by René Lacoste, a member of the famous 'French musketeers' and one of the great names of tennis history.

Basically nervous, Lacoste steeled himself always to appear calm—no matter what he felt inside. After a while friends constantly told him what a calm person he was. In the end he so believed it that he actually was calm.

Probably, however, the basic characteristics for calmness were already latent in Lacoste for one cannot instil into oneself or anyone else behaviour patterns which are basically alien.

This was proved during the war when brutalising courses for Commandos only succeeded in driving genetically timid men farther into their shells.

In post-war tennis I endeavoured to train one young starlet to become more dominating. As an exercise in this I dispatched her to a well-known restaurant with instructions to order a dish and, after its arrival, to call for the manager and make a fuss. She did, but the exercise failed to have the desired effect. By nature a gentle young woman, this was against her feelings and afterwards she was, if anything, even shyer than before. In a similar situation today, I would reason that 'mental domination' of the type displayed by a Fred Perry or Sven Davidson is out. She must seek perfection in the technical aspects of the game, be flooded with the desire to win and then she will do so by the sheer quality of her tennis.

Davidson provides a good example of a dominant personality.

When he, Jacques Brichant and Nicole Pietrangeli were battling for the top spot in European tennis, Davidson told me seriously and analytically 'no matter how badly I am playing, I can always beat them because I can dominate them mentally'.

Such power of personality is predominantly hereditary and can scarcely be acquired. The effects can sometimes be synthetised, as I found with Angela Buxton. She always found her friends outside tennis and, therefore, did not mind if she was considered stand-offish by her fellow competitors. Therefore she was set to study royalty in order to acquire an air of detached superiority. This perplexed and aggravated many potential opponents and, in consequence, distracted their minds from the task of playing good tennis; dislike or any personal emotion of that nature is, on the whole, a destroyer of peak technical performance.

It must be clearly understood that any recourse to on-court gamesmanship must be deplored. It is only a polite word for cheating, and cheating of any kind belittles the man or woman who offends. Only through seeking the best of which one is capable, both morally and technically, can one attain the full heights of self-respect. With self-respect one cannot tolerate anything but the best of which one is capable, whether it be on the tennis court or off.

Of course, 999 people out of 1,000 fall from grace from time to time; they wouldn't be human if they didn't. I am counselling seeking for perfection because I know that champions, in the year or years they become champions, do just that.

Maybe not in the abstract way in which I am discussing it here but certainly in the behaviour, training and practice senses.

At this point it might be as well to read Chapter 10 once more because the philosophical approach advocated therein may fairly be related to the psychological aspects now being covered.

One must seek always to maintain self-confidence and this is best achieved through positive action.

Some years ago *British Lawn Tennis* magazine researched into the on-court attitudes of a group of champions and discovered that all thoroughly disliked playing opponents who ran and ran and just kept returning the ball softly. Yet these players had all become champions by exploiting aggressive tennis.

This suggested that youngsters should be taught to defend like mad in each rally until the chance to hit a winner or force an opening arose. Then they should switch immediately to the attack.

This sounds fine in theory but on the court a negative safety-first attitude tends to be self-perpetuating so that only a man in a thousand can switch from soft to hard shots in rally after rally.

On the other hand a positive, point-seeking attitude tends to breed optimism and a sense of adventure—providing it is realistic and backed by sound technique.

This leads naturally to two differing thoughts which come into tennis players' minds.

One is, 'I must not lose this point.'

The other is, 'I have got to win this point.'

With the former thought a player usually surrenders the initiative to his opponent.

With the latter he takes the initiative even if the initiative is interpreted by running and running until the opponent breaks down.

In other words he is quite clear about how he is going to win the point in the end. And the value of being quite clear about how one is going to win a point is immense. In matches between good tournament players of comparable standards the man with sensible initiative carries a distinct advantage.

There remains the $64,000 question, what kind of animal embodies all the qualities postulated in this and the preceding chapters? What is the anatomy of a champion?

14

The Make-up of Champions

Medicos, psychologists, geneticists and their like mostly agree that man's character is determined by a mixture of heredity and environment. The only disagreements are on the relative importances of these factors.

So far as tennis is concerned, this puzzle relates very particularly to the discovery of potential champions and the development of this potentiality into actuality. It must be recognised that this has been very much a hit or miss business and, to date, I can think of only two English people other than myself who have approached early selection with a scientific attitude.

My own experiments have established to my complete satisfaction that character is more important than inherent ball sense, providing ball sense is not below a basic standard. This standard is by no means high—nothing like that of, say, Graham Stilwell or Gerald Battrick. My view is shared by Arthur Roberts, the man who discovered and developed Angela Mortimer and Mike Sangster.

Before analysing the self-assessments of twenty-one of the current world class champions and players, consider the remarks of a leading doctor-psychologist who has played for England and is a world authority in a game comparable in popularity to tennis; professional ethics prevent me revealing his name. He was the first scientist in those fields with whom I made contact. This was before the current scientific techniques of measuring personality, a more all-embracing term than character, had become known or accurate.

Later in this chapter I shall use a Cattell chart to blueprint my ideas of a champion's make-up. Meanwhile my colleague wrote ten years ago:

'The components of success are not just a straightforward equation of plus values. In any case, success is a by-product of activity which begets productiveness. The better the proficiency the better the success. Proficiency equals mental and physical capacity plus drive. And ambition nurtures drive. Ambition has no constitutional basis or background and is not hereditary. It is chiefly if not wholly environmental.'

Note that the doctor by implication rates ambition as a primary factor. 'Killer instinct' does not appear to enter into the reckoning and this is substantiated by the findings of a university research team who quizzed several hundred competitors during the 1958 Commonwealth and Empire Games at Cardiff. By an overwhelming majority those great champions denied any feeling of hate for their competitive opponents.

Cutting short any further development of this theme, one may assume that champions evolve out of ambition. Let it be noted here that very few current tennis players would be likely to recognise ambition in themselves.

What causes ambition? Ambition derives from having zest and love for something and doing it often enough to become indestructibly conditioned to that particular form of activity. The more you do it, the more you reach your full potentiality of purpose.

My small research covered twenty-one champions. Of these the following grew up in an environment which caused or developed their love for tennis and so, if the foregoing paragraphs are correct, nurtured ambition: Roy Emerson, Fred Stolle, Bob Hewitt, Margaret Court, Jan Lehane, Karen Susman, Nancy Richey, Billie-Jean King, Abe Segal, Renée Haygarth, Rafael Osuna, Tony Palafox, Bob Wilson, Nicole Pietrangeli, Maria Bueno and Ken Rosewall.

Angela Mortimer and Mike Sangster were exposed to special and favourable environmental conditions slightly later than most players; Nikola Pilic and Wilhelm Bungert I am not sure

I*   131

about. Only Chuck McKinley evolved from a hostile (to tennis) environment in which he literally had fist fights with other boys who denigrated tennis.

Each of these twenty-one players was asked to list the five most important factors in their success. Between them they listed forty-seven factors.

Two stood far out from all others, namely physical condition and concentration. Concentration was named by fourteen of the twenty-one, peak physical condition by thirteen.

It is worth noting here that during the making of the Nestlé-Slazenger film on service, Rosewall was asked: 'If you had to make the choice between peak physical condition and a big service, which would you pick?' The then world champion answered: 'Peak physical condition.'

In giving this answer all thirteen may be presumed to have embraced speed and stamina. However, five players—Emerson, Margaret Court, McKinley, Osuna and Bungert—listed speed separately while Bungert also registered the solitary separate vote for stamina.

Six players reckoned luck had played an important part in careers, namely Emerson, Hewitt, Jan Lehane, McKinley, Karen Susman and Osuna.

Two players only—both women—named dedication.

Guts, determination and will to win should, I feel, be lumped together so far as these questionnaires were concerned. They tallied five—Margaret Court, Jan Lehane, Nancy Richey, Angela Mortimer and Billie-Jean King.

Technicalities played a very minor part in the answers, Stolle naming eye on the ball and position of feet, Palafox and Bungert stipulating timing.

Hewitt and Jan Lehane consider they possess good big match temperaments, Ken Rosewall and Nancy Richey nominated keenness. Here environment can be seen creeping in, because Rosewall used to be bundled into his pram along with his parents' rackets, and he was expert on a practice wall by the time he was five years old; Nancy Richey is the daughter of a very enthusiastic tennis coach.

Some of the players came up with unusual reasons for parts

132

of their success. Renée Haygarth is affected by her mood and starting right. Nikola Pilic, a university student, believes his way of life has helped him. Bungert is sparked by personal satisfaction in playing well. Pietrangeli likes crowd support and named the wish to be respected by other players, to please his family and to do good for his country's tennis as the other factors in his success. Emerson gave fundamental happiness as his most important factor. Happily married and with children he clearly adores, settled in a job which pays well and offers a future, there was no happier player than Emerson in 1964. And just look at his results. Billie-Jean King stakes much on religious faith.

Viewed as a whole, the answers were surprising and not, I feel, particularly accurate.

What is significant is that only one player, Hewitt, rated ability a factor in his success. From this one may fairly imply that the champions believe that natural ability is secondary compared to a number of other aspects of tennis.

Maria Bueno alone used the term genius, adding the rider 'working'. The general opinion contradicts this and seems to be, bending a phrase, 'tennis success comes from 10 per cent inspiration and 90 per cent perspiration'.

Well, anyone can work intelligently and hard, so if you are not a 'natural' do not despair. The stars, twenty of them anyway, believe you can succeed in spite of this.

Those, then, are the views of twenty-one very successful practitioners in the game. Let me take this a stage further by relating all that has gone before to a scientific hypothesis for the personality of a champion.

I shall use the Cattell sixteen personality factor system. Those who wish to delve further into this should obtain a copy of the July 1965 issue of *British Lawn Tennis* magazine. They should also read *The Scientific Analysis of Personality* by Raymond B. Cattell (Pelican Books).

The Cattell chart places a subject somewhere along a ten-point scale which stretches between the two extremes of each measured factor, e.g. tough versus tender-minded, dull versus intelligent, assurance versus guilt-proneness, etc.; the average man will come out somewhere between 4·75 and 6·25 approximately on all factors.

Understand, the number is not a score—merely a co-ordinate, a position. Thus a score of 5·5 on the factor tough versus tender-minded indicates an exact balance between the two extremes.

What kind of factors would one expect to find in a champion if the substance of this book is correct?

Eventually I will show the complete chart of one of the world's great players of the past decade. The questionnaire was completed in confidence so the identity of the player—it may be a man or a woman—cannot be revealed. To avoid grammatical complications I will name the player X and make use of the masculine gender throughout.

Though a great player, X cannot be described as a natural genius in the manner of, say, Maureen Connolly. His success seemingly sprang from a number of slightly above average attributes plus great persistence.

To revert to the Cattell 16 PF system, the first factor concerns warmth and sociability at one end of the scale, aloofness and stiffness at the other. It is a component in the second order extroversion-introversion factor and we know that introversion and persistence tend to go together. However, most stars possess good—not outstanding—natural ability which often links with extroversion, so our expectation is of an average reading.

The second factor is roughly comparable to I.Q. and here I have good news for those who may secretly feel they are a little on the dull side.

Neither at school, nor at Wimbledon champion level can there be found any correlation between I.Q. and motor skill. A research carried out in London comprehensive schools showed a completely random 'scatter' and this relates perfectly with the research carried out by *British Lawn Tennis* magazine into the personalities of tennis champions.

The third factor, emotional stability or instability, appears vital, for this reflects one's conception of self and one's attitude to life. In Freudian language, it is a measure of ego strength. One seldom finds fanatics among champions, but strength in this vital factor is necessary.

The fourth continuum stretches from aggressive competitiveness to kindly mildness. Seemingly this should be high, but not so high as to eliminate all enjoyment from the activity undertaken or to overwhelm the humility necessary for learning.

Factor five, 'F' on the chart, is surgency versus desurgency—'get up and go' against languidness. There must be a goodly slice of this in the make-up. Factor G comes nearest to the popular idea of 'character' and is predominantly inherited. On the one hand it shows perseverance, determination and conscientiousness, on the other indolence, quitting, demanding, impatience.

So one looks for a high score but bewares of excess, for this in all factors suggests imbalance.

Factor H relates venturesomeness to timidity. Too much means a carefree, unthinking attitude, too little a tendency to over-caution. Tennis, one theorises, needs slightly more than average venturesomeness.

Factor I is toughness versus sensitivity and tender-mindedness, and there is no room for the latter in tennis. However, imagination is a necessary virtue, both on the competitive court and when practising; remember mental rehearsal and retroactive inhibition.

Therefore, one tempers the immediate idea of excessive toughness while still seeking an above average reading.

Factor L relates open-mindedness, willingness to take a chance, composure and cheerfulness with suspicion, hardness and irritability.

Factor M covers the extremes of practicality and Bohemianism.

Factor N is concerned with sophistication versus *naïveté*.

Without delving into reasons, I believe that midway positions in all these factors are best suited to itinerant tennis stars.

Factor O is extremely vital for it covers the basic inner security of a person. A poor rating on this is terribly dangerous for it forewarns of the over-anxious unreliable performances which all of us have found so difficult to understand in a number of nearly-outstanding stars.

Only exceptional strengths can compensate for genetic plus

135

environmental-bred insecurity so one looks for a low score here.

The Q factors 1 and 2 cover radicalism versus conservatism and self-sufficiency versus group dependency. Average positions appear right.

Q3 and Q4 both contribute to general anxiety, the former because of self-control or lack of it, the latter because it measures what might simply be called 'raggety nerves'.

One looks for good self-control but not complete nerveless-ness; a champion should show some ergic tension, to give it its technical term.

Before showing this personally postulated conception of a champion's make-up compared with the actual make-up of X and that of fifteen of the world's top players of 1964–5, let me add one or two riders.

Firstly, no man or woman is likely to coincide exactly with such an ideal conception.

Secondly, I do not believe one should wish for or find a 1 or 10 position on any factor because this suggests poor balance.

Thirdly, the letters on the Cattell 16 PF chart leave some blank spaces. These letters are part of an internationally recognised code.

Now for the combined chart, Figure 24.

It shows that actual champion X corresponds very closely with my postulated champion.

The fact that X rates stronger on surgency and super ego strength and is tougher, more self-assured and more forthright could be expected.

X's scores on Q3 and Q4 are a shade surprising and indicate reasons for failures in lesser events where incentives have not been great.

What everyday signs should my postulated champion show of possessing the necessary qualities?

It would take another book to enumerate all of them, so here are just a few.

He would tend to be more interested in people than abstract ideas. No sleep will be lost over trivial worries, or serious regrets harboured over past deeds. He will be slightly conforming and obedient and possibly somewhat softly spoken.

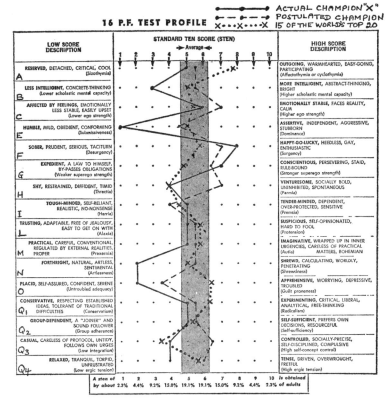

FIGURE 24

There could be a certain amount of 'ham acting' in his behaviour and perhaps a liking for excitement.

He will be loyal to his friends and painstakingly thorough in any tasks he undertakes.

He may seem a little wrapped up in his own thoughts at times and will have a few close friends rather than a wide circle of shallow acquaintances.

There will be signs of leadership and practicality and an unwillingness to let shoddy service go by unchallenged.

Tolerance he will possess quite noticeably; also reasonable optimism. He will disregard small ailments, perhaps to the point of danger to himself. He will ride criticism easily.

137

He will like to hear both sides of an argument and will usually be on the look-out to learn. He will have the digestion of an ostrich.

He may be slightly absent-minded and casual but is not likely to get rattled very easily.

Though a good sleeper he may have the occasional disturbed night. He will not be easily distracted but may occasionally show restlessness for no apparent reason.

Bear in mind that these are only a few clues to tendencies, and that in most cases my use of the word 'will' is too strong.

When assessing a youngster, too, one must look for a good quota of 'get up and go'.

Technically, anyone with ambition must have good balance, co-ordination, sense of timing and some natural grace of movement. A youngster is likely to show marked inventiveness, especially in games played with a ball and wall.

He will also be persistent in seeking fitness.

Yet over and above all these factors there are two which are ultimately decisive; ambition and a real love of tennis.

The former keeps one striving intelligently and purposefully for improvement, for revenge over the conqueror of last week, for a special event next month.

Love of tennis gives one sheer animal joy in just being out on the court, running around and hitting the ball well.

These attitudes are rewards in themselves, almost irrespective of any other considerations. Yet it is strange how often they lead on to attainment.

So to the aspiring champion I finally counsel—aim at enjoyment, perfection and fitness, and you will be giving yourself the best chance of ultimate success.

And with the British game thrown open to amateurs and professionals alike by the new rule 30 introduced on 22nd April 1968 by the Lawn Tennis Association, financial success too . . . but that is another story.

Motivation of Champions

As part of the research it is carrying out with tennis players, *British Lawn Tennis* magazine issued an exploratory questionnaire to a group of well-known circuit players (all current competitors).

The breakdown was as follows:

CATEGORY 1. Nine players, men and women, who have either won or have been runners-up in one or more events in one of the four major championships (Wimbledon, France, America and Australia).

CATEGORY 2. Winners of open international championships (12 players).

CATEGORY 3. Winners of senior national championships (6 players).

CATEGORY 4. Winners of national junior championships (10 players).

CATEGORY 5. Tournament players (16 players).

Because the questionnaire was exploratory, some of the questions turned out to be of little or no value. In studying answers, too, the analyst must make mental reservations for some self-deceit in the people being questioned.

Nevertheless, the answers to some questions shed interesting light on the make-up of many players whose names are known throughout the world. The questions were:

(3) What is your secret ambition? (*a*) To win Wimbledon; (*b*) to play in the Davis Cup/Wightman Cup/Federation Cup; (*c*) to play at Wimbledon; (*d*) to play for your county; (*e*) to win club championship; (*f*) to have fun and meet people.

(4) Within your inner heart, how do you rate your chances of achieving your ambition? (*a*) Excellent; (*b*) very good; (*c*) fair; (*e*) remote.

(8) Why do you wish to become a great player? (*a*) I don't; (*b*) I enjoy fame; (*c*) it will be financially rewarding or help me to get a good job; (*d*) to please my parents and friends; (*f*) personal satisfaction and achievement.

The answers given by each category to question 3 (answer in capital letter) and to question 4 (small letter) in player categories were:

1		2		3		4		5	
A	b	A	e	B	b	A	b	E	b
B	a	A	c	B	c	B	b	A	e
B	a	F	d	A	d	B	a	E	d
A	d	F	d	A	c	BA	bd	C	d
A	d	B	d	A	e	B	b	A	a
B	a	A	a	A	c	B	d	B	a
A	c	B	d			B	f	B	d
F	a	A	b			B	d	A	c
F	c	B	b			C	d	B	d
		A	c			A	c	F	b
		None						A	e
		A	c					CB	aa
								C	d
								C	d
								C	c
								B	d

The answers of category 1 amplify as five of the nine players have won the singles at one of the big four championships and all have played Davis, Wightman or Federation Cup tennis. Yet winning Wimbledon is only just ahead of playing cup tennis as an ambition while one winner of a major singles plays only to have fun and meet people.

140

The answer to question 8 shows that an overwhelming number of those questioned claim they wish to become great (or wished in the case of category 1 and 2 for personal satisfaction).

These categories include some of the players commanding the biggest expenses obtainable, but six—none in category 1—answered that it will be or is financially rewarding. The full schedule of answers was (some players gave more than one reason):

1	2	3	4	5
DEF	F	F	F	FBC
DF	F	FC	FC	F
F	E	BE	F	F
F	E	F	FCD	BCDE
F	F	F	FD	E
F	C	None	F	F
DEF	F		EF	F
F	F		F	C
E	F		D	EF
	F		DEF	A
	F			F
				F
				A
				F
				F

If the answers were given sincerely, and everything points to the fact that they were, the popular idea that amateurs are motivated by the thought of the huge expenses that they can earn seems in need of closer examination.

Question 11 provided a far more significant set of answers. It ran: You are at school. If offered the choice, which do you pick? (*a*) A place at University? (*b*) Three years on the tennis circuit?

The answers were:

CATEGORY 1: 3 university, 4 circuit, 1 both, 1 no answer.
CATEGORY 2: 7 university, 5 circuit.
CATEGORY 3: 1 university, 4 circuit, 1 no answer.
CATEGORY 4: 1 university, 9 circuit
CATEGORY 5: 4 university, 9 circuit, 1 both, 2 no answer.

The average ages of the categories show that the players in 1 and 2 have had a longer period to reach their higher playing standards. The average ages are:

CATEGORY 1. 25·1   CATEGORY 2. 24·5   CATEGORY 3·20
CATEGORY 4. 19·4   CATEGORY 5. 21·66.

Adding together the two higher attainment categories gives 10 opting for a university place, 9 for three years on the circuit.

The other, lower attainment, lower age groups when aggregated score 6 university, 22 circuit.

Unquestionably the sample is too small to be in any way conclusive—yet the contrast in the figures is too clear cut to be ignored.

Is it simply that the extra years have saturated the older, better players with tennis and they yearn for other things?

Category 1 includes four players who are very recent winners of a French Singles Championship, reputedly the toughest event in the world in terms of sheer hard work. Of that four, three answered question 11 with 'three years on the circuit'. The other (most talented but least hard working) chose 'university'.

This could be a small clue to unequivocal love of tennis, above all else, breeding success but, again, the sample is minute.

This idea is supplemented by the answers of Category 1 to question 13: how much do you expect to be earning at the age of thirty?

This group includes several of those who draw very high expenses today. Except in the case of those with an American environment, their expected earnings are modest; in several cases probably less than they are currently drawing in 'expenses' as 'amateurs'.

To repeat, the questionnaire was exploratory and any theories based on the findings from this small sample must be treated with the utmost reserve. Nevertheless, it does produce some evidence suggesting that very successful players are motivated by an uncomplicated love of the game itself and that other factors are lower in importance. Sheer love of tennis as a primary, powerful driving force has been strangely overlooked in post-war British tennis.

Training for Lawn Tennis

The following programme is designed to give the player a basic physical fitness without which he cannot attain his full potential as a player, regardless of the amount of talent he has. It is not a substitute for playing practice on the court and is complementary to learning the skills of the game.

Remember that it is better to do physical training 'a little and often' rather than to train for long periods at irregular intervals. The first method can be enjoyed, the second tends to discourage further efforts. The following exercises are designed to increase your speed, strength and stamina—the three basic requirements of physical fitness. They require a minimum of equipment and need no special skill to perform.

THE EXERCISES

(1) *Bench Steps.* Step on to a bench (low enough to reach without undue effort) and off again. Legs must be straightened when on the bench. Lead with left leg for half number repetitions. Right leg for other half.

(2) *Trunk Curls* (lying). Flat on back with hands clasped behind head. Keeping legs straight bend up to touch knees with forehead.

(3) *Press-Ups.* Front support position on finger-tips. Keeping the whole body straight bend and straighten arms.

(4) *Chest Raising.* Lying face downwards with hands clasped behind back, arms straight. Lift head, shoulders and chest off floor.

(5) *Toe Touching.* Stand with legs apart. Keeping legs straight,

touch the ground outside feet, in front of you and through legs then back to vertical.

(6) *Double Knee Jumps.* Stand on toes, with feet together. Leap up and bound knees against chest and back to starting position.

(7) *Chin Heave.* Stand beneath a bar that you can just grip with arms straight. Pull up until chin is level with bar, then lower and bounding off the ground between heaves.

(8) *Vertical Punch.* Holding dumb-bell (or a brick) in each hand start from arms back position. Punch alternate arms vertically.

(9) *Skipping.* Vary the skipping steps and work as fast as possible.

(10) *Interval Running.* Jog along slowly for 50 yds, then sprint for 20 yds.

HOW TO USE THESE EXERCISES

(1) CIRCUIT TRAINING

(*a*) Select nine or ten exercises from the list—do not include Interval Running which should be done after completing circuit training and, if possible, on non-circuit days.

(*b*) At the first session perform each exercise in turn for 30 seconds (or until you can do no more) and record the number of repetitions done. This is your TEST RATE. It is important to go through the full range of movement at each exercise. To get your TRAINING RATE at each exercise, halve the TEST RATE.

(*c*) At the second session perform each exercise at the TRAINING RATE. Then repeat so that you have performed each exercise twice. Time yourself from the start of the first exercise to the end of the last one. Record time taken. After a short rest commence Interval Running for 5—10 minutes.

(*d*) Third, fourth, fifth and sixth session as for second session.

(*e*) Seventh and all subsequent sessions—Do the circuit three times instead of two at same Training Rate.

(*f*) Record the total time taken for each session. After several weeks you should notice that the time has been reduced. When the margin by which it is reduced each session becomes only a

145

few seconds or when you cannot reduce it at all it is time to re-test your capacity as in (*b*) above. You should find that your TEST RATE has risen as a result of the work you have done. This is positive proof that you are now fitter.

(*g*) Use a chart like the one attached to record your progress.

(2) GENERAL

(*a*) Train as above at least twice a week but preferably three times. (However, if you are doing similar work regularly in the gym at school, then you will not need to do this programme as often. The best person to advise you about this is your Physical Education Master at school or whoever is supervising your training.)

(*b*) Always get thoroughly warm before starting circuit training by spending a few minutes jogging round a track (or road) and doing a few limbering up exercises. It is important to get the blood flowing in the muscles which you are about to exercise.

(*c*) Do not be surprised if the first two or three sessions leave you feeling stiff the following day. In fact if you do not feel stiff you are probably not doing the exercises properly. A few minutes spent limbering up will soon remove the stiffness.

(*d*) Training done as suggested above in competition with your own past performance and the clock can be enjoyable. But remember that training is not an end in itself; its purpose is to make you better equipped, both physically and mentally, to play better tennis.

No.	EXERCISE	Date		TRNG RATE	Date		TRNG RATE	Date		TRNG RATE
		Test			Test			Test		
1.										
2.										
3.										
4.										
5.										
6.										
7.										
8.										
9.										
0.										

ATE	TIME TAKEN	DATE	TIME TAKEN	DATE	TIME TAKEN	DATE	TIME TAKEN	DATE	TIME TAKEN

'73 **Date Due**

MY 11 '73			
AG 29 '75			
DE 19 '78			
FE 16 '77			
NO 5			
JY 30 '82			
NOV 23 '83			
NO 8 '97			
NOV 3 0 2008			

Demco 38-297